STEREO HANDBOOK

STEREO HANDBOOK

G. W. SCHANZ

DRAKE PUBLISHERS INC
NEW YORK 1972

ISBN. 87749-003-1

Published 1972
Drake Publishers, Inc.
381 Park Avenue South,
New York, N.Y. 10016.

Printed in The Netherlands.

PREFACE

In recent years Stereophony has found a continuously expanding field of application and is now always considered in close relation to methods of recording, reproducing and transmitting sound. It is therefore essential that those involved professionally or otherwise should gain an understanding of the subject. Although there is no shortage of literature dealing with this matter, the present paperback on Stereophony is intended only to give a brief survey, to facilitate understanding and, last but not least, to give useful directions for the appropriate testing of stereo reproduction equipment.

The reader will no doubt understand that the scope of a paperback is essentially limited, and one cannot expect it to provide all the answers. This Stereophony paperback has been designed expressly to give an explanation of the most important principles to a circle of readers consisting mainly of technicians and stereo enthusiasts. With this as a basis no further serious difficulties should arise.

G. W. Schanz

CONTENTS

CHAPTER 1

FUNDAMENTALS OF STEREOPHONIC SOUND PERCEPTION

It is indeed remarkable that in this modern age a great deal of thought is being devoted to something which has been a human faculty ever since the creation of man: stereophonic sound perception. It may be partly due to our modern way of living that this particular faculty, highly important to primitive man, has to some extent been 'forgotten'. Originally auditory perspective was a faculty warning man of impending danger or assisting him in his search for food [1]. Such warning and assistance were all the more valuable if at the same time they gave some indication of where the danger lay or his prey was to be found. Even today, and especially in dense traffic, the warning function of auditory perspective is something we could not do without.

One might be led to believe that stereophonic sound perception has only recently become a centre of interest in sound transmission. The idea is, however, not at all new [1]. As early as 1550 the Dutch composer Adriaan Willaert conceived the idea of two separate choirs, one on each side of the church. Baroque organs were built in separate sections which were installed at different points and according to their respective positions were termed *Great Organ*, *Swell Organ*, *Choir Organ*, *Solo Organ*, etc. Then there was Berlioz who at the first performance of his Requiem in the Dôme Des Invalides positioned four complete orchestras in the four corners of the Dôme to symbolise the angels at the four corners of the earth, summoning the souls of the departed to judgement.

When considering the many possibilities of recording, amplifying and reproducing sound, technicians often overlook the most important factor: the listener for whose ear the sound is after all intended [2]. All this is based on a historical development showing the close relation between electro-acoustics and physiological acoustics.

Problems on which interest is now concentrated, and collectively termed 'Hi-Fi', were already being studied many years ago. However, before Stereophony had found its way into Electro-acoustics, people had to be satisfied with monaural sound transmission. In this connection endeavours were made to eliminate the so-called 'hole-in-the-wall' effect caused by using one loudspeaker only. Fig. 1.1 is an example of how this can be done in a living room [3]. The sound installation comprises a corner cabinet with two bass loudspeakers, two separate cabinets with a double-cone loudspeaker for middle and high notes as well as a frequency filter dividing the tone spectrum into one range above 420 c/s, and another below 420 c/s. Sound diffusion can be obtained by appropriate positioning of the treble loudspeaker so that the listener will perceive mainly indirect sound. In this way the conditions in a concert hall can be imitated while at the same time the 'hole-in-the-wall' effect is eliminated.

Fig. 1.1. Loudspeaker arrangement to eliminate the 'hole-in-the-wall' effect. The arrows indicate the three loudspeaker cabinets

This in itself provides proof that we have in fact always had stereophonic sound perception in mind. The fact that we had to diffuse sound to give our ears the impression of receiving stereophonic sound need not necessarily be qualified as deception, since monophonic installations also failed to give faithful sound reproduction. In the course of time a home studio technique [4] known as 'Hi-Fi' developed parallel with stereophony.

Technicians and others seriously interested in these techniques need not be concerned by the fact that expressions like 'Stereo' and 'Hi-Fi' have practically become household words. It is far more important to realise that there must be close association between the two if satisfactory results are to be obtained. Therefore it is essential to know something about the principles of stereophonic hearing.

By 'stereophonic' hearing is understood that sound 'not coming from a point source' is perceived by both ears in such a way as to give an impression of 'space'. It is the opposite of 'monophonic' sound perception which is hearing with both ears sound emanating from a point source. This must not be confused with 'monaural' and 'binaural' sound perception. For these terms are used to indicate that hearing takes place with 'one' or 'two' ears respectively. The former is the case when a person with one deaf ear perceives sound. Similarly, if sound is recorded with one microphone only we speak of *monaural recording*. This implies by no means that the reproduction of the sound is also monaural; for it can be heard with two ears, a process termed *monophonic reproduction*.

1.1 Directional hearing

The basis of this 'new' development is in fact the age old faculty of directional hearing. It goes right to the heart of the matter when we read in a prospectus [5]: 'Man is naturally equipped for 'stereophony' '. Of course the average person takes it for granted that he can find his way about in his acoustic world. What else could he do? On the other hand, however, to gain insight into stereophony we must also study directional hearing.

In the first place it must be realised that stereophony is much more than just a means for performing tricks [6]. No doubt the reader has more than once noticed that his ears do not merely perceive sound, but also can distinguish from what direction the sound is coming. If a person is addressed he automatically turns to the speaker. With eyes closed one can, for instance, tell that a motorcar or tram is approaching from the left to continue its way to the right. We hear all the sounds round us with 'two' ears, each one registering sound independently of the other.

Thus the human ear has particular qualities which are indispensable for judging sound and sound impressions [7]. In the first place there is sensitivity, which is highly frequency dependent, as explained in Fig. 1.2 [8]. The curves shown there are termed 'hearing curves' or 'isophones'. The hearing curve for 0 dB marks the threshold of hearing. Note also that the curves flatten as the sound becomes louder, which indicates that the frequency dependency becomes less pronounced. The frequency response for the human ear ranges from about 20 to 20,000 c/s. The higher limit particularly varies with age; the sensitivity to higher frequencies weakens considerably as one grows older.

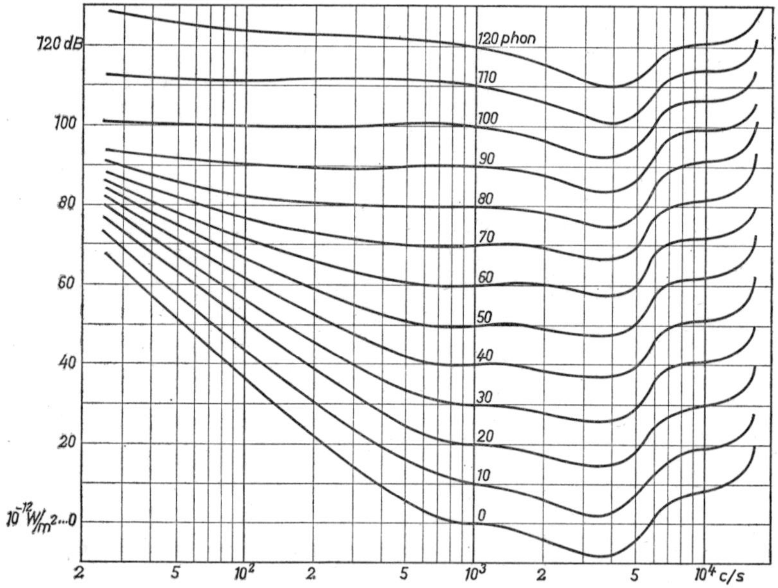

Fig. 1.2. Hearing curves at equal sound levels

At sound levels slightly exceeding 120 phon the sensitivity of the ear approaches the pain level. A sound standard has been established to investigate and record hearing qualities [7]. The method is based on what is known as 'volume comparison'. A reference tone of 1,000 c/s is made to give a sound impression equal to that of the sound under investigation. Apart from that there are other requirements which must be met. The sound intensity is expressed in how many phons the reference sound is then above the hearing threshold (0 phon). Table 1.1 below gives a clear example for various sound levels [9]. One phon corresponds to one decibel in the sound scale ($1 \cdot 10^{-16}$ W/cm^2) relative to a sound pressure ($2 \cdot 10^{-4}$ μbar) at 1,000 c/s. This is a good approximation between about 700 and 1,800 c/s. For the remaining frequencies corresponding values can be found in Fig. 1.2.

TABLE 1.1

phons	Sound sources
130	Threshold of pain
120	Airplane at distance of 3 m; kettle drum at a distance of 1 m
110	Boiler riveting
100	Motorcycles without a silencer
90	Pneumatic hammer and car horns at 1 m
80	Noisy factory hall; shouting at 1 m
70	Loud speech; noisy streets, noisy loudspeakers
60	Normal loudspeaker
50	Quiet street; conversation at 1 m
40	Tearing paper at 1 m
30	Normal whispering at 1 m
20	Quiet garden; ticking clock; fine rain
10	Rustle of leaves; soft whispering at 3 m
0	Threshold of hearing

Bearing the foregoing in mind, there is a risk that too hasty a conclusion may be come to in finding close relations between directional hearing and sound intensity. Originally, directional hearing was explained in terms of intensity ratios and differences [1]. If a source of sound is located asymmetrically with respect to the head of the observer, there is indeed a difference between the sound impressions received by the two ears. This is partly due to damping caused by the side of the head turned towards the sound source, and partly to the fact that the ear turned away from the source is screened off by the head. As a rule the difference in sound intensity increases as the sound source is further distantiated from the plane of symmetry through the head.

It has been found, however, that the difference does not depend solely on the angle between the direction of the sound source and the plane of symmetry of the head, but is also strongly influenced by the sound impression itself. For low frequency notes there is hardly any difference in perception between the two ears. For pure high pitched notes, however, the difference can be really striking. This is illustrated in Fig. 1.3. There, the intensity differences between the two ears are shown, as occurring when the ambient sound is emitted by a source producing purely sinusoidal tones. If, however, the sounds vary constantly, as is the case, for instance, in normal conversation, so will the intensity perceived by each ear. It will then be convenient to speak of an average intensity variation.

There is still another factor involved in directional hearing: the time element, that is to say the difference in time needed for a sound to reach

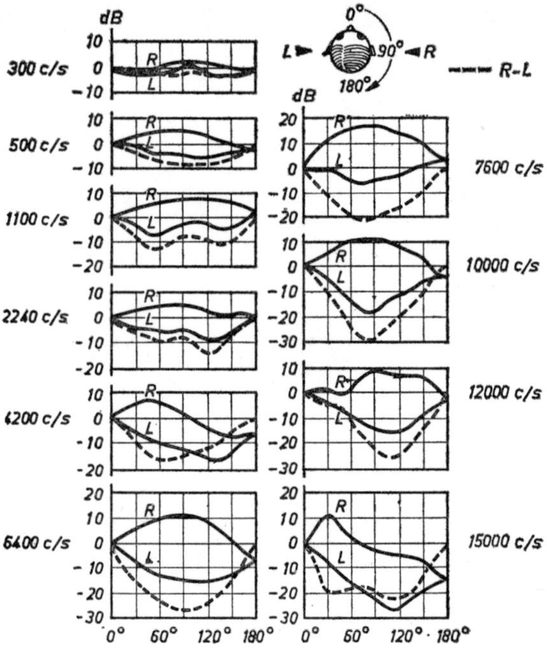

Fig. 1.3. Variations in intensity are not only determined by the angle between the direction of the sound source and the plane of symmetry of the head, but also by the nature of the particular sound

both ears. The cause lies in the unequal distances of the source with respect to either ear. Consequently time and intensity differences occur practically always simultaneously in directional hearing. This has been confirmed by investigation [1, 10].

Of course the main factor in directional hearing is the location of the source. The orientating faculty of the ears, together with the ability of locating sound sources applies to all three dimensions [11]. In accordance with the three dimensions there are

Depth perception = Distance to the sound source
Height perception = In the direction of the vertical plane of symmetry
Lateral perception = In the direction of the horizontal plane of symmetry.

Both depth and height perception are of hardly any importance for directional hearing. In depth perception it was found that when hearing sound in the open we can locate the source by the colour change of the sound. One must, however, know what the original sound is like as otherwise correct judgement of the distance becomes doubtful. Where continuous tones or even explosions are concerned it is hardly possible to judge the distance correctly. When perceiving sound in rooms, the impression of distance is moreover greatly dependent on the ratio between direct and indirect sound. The larger a room, the more the feeling for distance will be lost, particularly when the source is far away.

The faculty of auditory height perception is equally imperfect. Observations have proved that by tilting the head, vertical directional perception is reduced to mainly lateral auditory perception in the horizontal plane of symmetry. Vertical auditory perception can be greatly affected by visual impressions [8]. An example is the ceiling loudspeakers in theatres and cinemas, serving to reproduce the ringing of bells, air-raid alarm etc. In these cases the acoustic effects, which are most important, are supported by the scene on stage or screen.

Lateral perception is the main factor in directional sound perception. Here, the two ears function together in a horizontal plane. In this connection the differences in time and loudness with which sound reaches the ears are the main factors, and normal hearing is quite capable of noticing such differences.

1.2 Room acoustics

As stereophony finds its widest field of application in rooms it is important for the stereo technician to become acquainted with room acoustics. It is no exaggeration to say that for a number of years now the quality of electrical sound and speech reproduction has been so high that even experts and critical listeners have hardly been able to differentiate them from the originals [8]. Another important milestone in the development of electro-acoustics was reached when famous musicians not only allowed loudspeakers and accessories to be mounted in the concert hall, but even welcomed them as a means for lending their performances a special quality which they would otherwise be denied [12].

For the discussions in Section 1.1 it was assumed that by controlling sound at the source, it could be made to travel over greater distances. Walls enclosing living rooms, concert halls and the like limit propagation of sound waves. The energy of the sound waves is partly reflected by the walls and partly absorbed [1,8]. The audience seated in a room receives but a small part of the sound from the source ('direct sound'). By far the greater part heard by the audience is 'indirect sound', i.e. sound reflected by the walls. Consequently speech and music sound much louder in rooms than in the open where, owing to the absence of sound reflectors, only direct sound can be heard.

Direct sound is characteristic of the source. It embodies the actual information, the real artistic quality of the performance. It is thanks to auditory perspective that listeners can, for instance, acoustically perceive in direct sound the expanse of an orchestra and the movements of actors on the stage. For sound reproduction this implies that to obtain satisfactory results the loudspeakers must reproduce 'direct' sound with its 'natural' spectrum and dynamics in a 'stereophonically correct' way.

Although 'indirect' sound is produced by the same source, it is primarily characteristic of the 'acoustics of the room'. There are three points of difference between direct and indirect sound. In the first place, indirect sound does not come from one single direction, but from all directions. Indirect sound is therefore said to be 'diffuse'. This diffusion of sound will be the more pronounced as the walls reflect more sound in all directions and sound absorption is low. As indirect sound is diffuse sound, it will be almost equally loud in all parts of the room.

Another difference is that, owing to reflections, indirect sound travels a greater distance than direct sound and is, therefore, always somewhat 'delayed' to an extent which depends on the conditions of the room concerned. But even a short delay of reflected sound is sufficient to mask or even eliminate directional hearing by means of the direct sound.

The third difference is that direct sound disappears almost immediately when the source becomes silent. Indirect sound, however, lingers on for a certain time. How long that will be depends on how much of the sound is absorbed at each reflection from the walls. Furthermore, sound is damped while propagated through air. This damping or attenuation increases with the sound frequency. The lower the absorption, the louder and more diffuse will be the resultant sound, and also the longer before silence is restored.

These phenomena are characterised by the 'reverberation time' which is the time which elapses between the instant at which the source is silenced and that at which the sound has fallen to one millionth part of the initial intensity or to one thousandth part of the initial pressure [7]. Fig. 1.4 shows the maximum reverberation time for different sounds in relation to the volume of the room.

Generally the reverberation time increases with the volume of the room as the volume increases faster than the total area of the walls. These are empirically determined values for maximum reverberation, depending on the volume of the room and the kind of sound produced. The graphs of Fig. 1.4

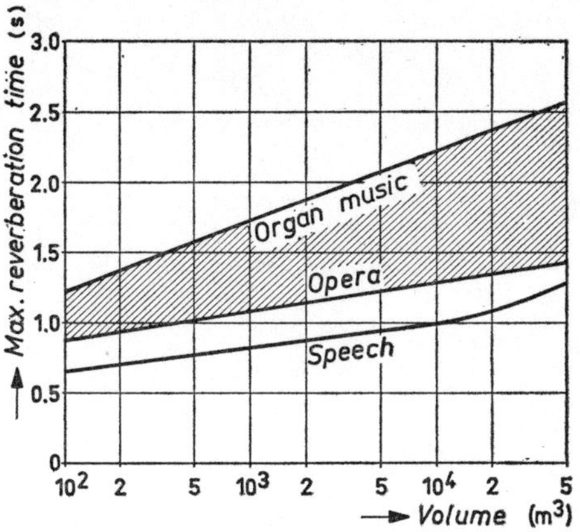

Fig. 1.4. Maximum reverberation times for various kinds of sound plotted against the volume of the room

apply to a frequency of 500 c/s. The degree of absorption of the different materials used for the walls is, however, 'frequency dependent'. Consequently each room or hall will have its own individual 'tone colour'. In this respect there is, for instance, a great difference between a wooden and a brick structure. A room with a glass roof or containing large windows will have a short reverberation time for low frequencies as the glass will mainly transmit this frequency. Furthermore the audience in a hall accounts for a considerable amount of absorption. To ensure that the acoustics of such halls are not highly dependent on the number of public the chairs are, for instance, upholstered in a material rendering absorption of the empty hall practically the same as if all seats were occupied. The most favourable frequency dependency of the reverberation time for any particular kind of performance can be selected by suitable treatment as shown in Fig. 1.5. The reverberation time at 500 c/s forms the unit. We already know that the reverberation times for lower frequencies are somewhat larger; a fact following from the properties of the human ear (see Fig. 1.2).

If the reverberation time is not in accordance with the desired values, corrections can be made by changing the covering of the walls. Generally the reverberation time for low frequencies is too long, and for high frequencies often too short. The cause is to be found in the porosity of most building

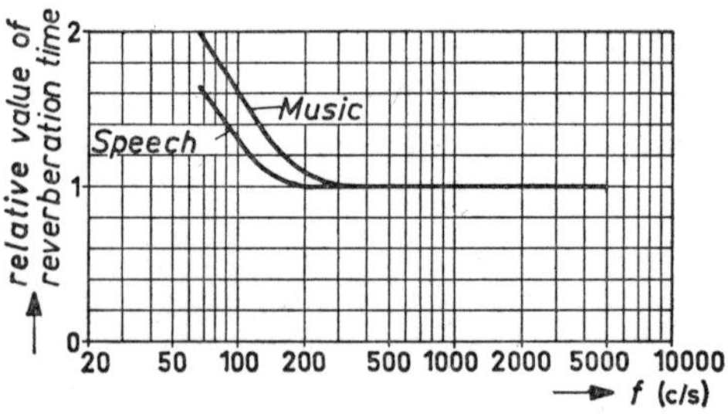

Fig. 1.5. Most favourable frequency dependency of the reverberation time depending on the type of performance given

materials. In the pores and channels running through the materials sound is converted into heat caused by friction. At the same time absorption of these materials increases with frequency. Table 1.2 shows the absorption coefficients of various materials [7].

TABLE 1.2

Material	128 c/s	512 c/s	2048 c/s
Tiled wall, rough	0.024	0.03	0.05
Tiled wall, smooth	0.024	0.06	0.06
Parquet	0.03	0.06	0.10
Linoleum	0.02	0.03	0.04
Glass	0.04	0.03	0.02
Wood panelling	0.09	0.17	0.15
Plywood (20 mm from wall)	0.07	0.28	0.10
Carpet (10 mm on bare floor)	0.09	0.21	0.27
Carpet (10 mm on 3 mm underfelt)	0.11	0.37	0.27
Curtain	0.07	0.49	0.66
Public (normal seating) (per m^2)	0.72	0.95	1.00

This table clearly shows that absorption is indeed frequency dependent. A better illustration is perhaps given in Fig. 1.6 in which, in accordance with Table 1.2, the frequency dependency is expressed in percentage [13]. It now becomes more apparent that there are methods of changing the acoustic qualities of a room by an appropriate choice of material.

By means of Fig. 1.5 it has already been pointed out that each type of performance requires its own 'most favourable' reverberation time. It would,

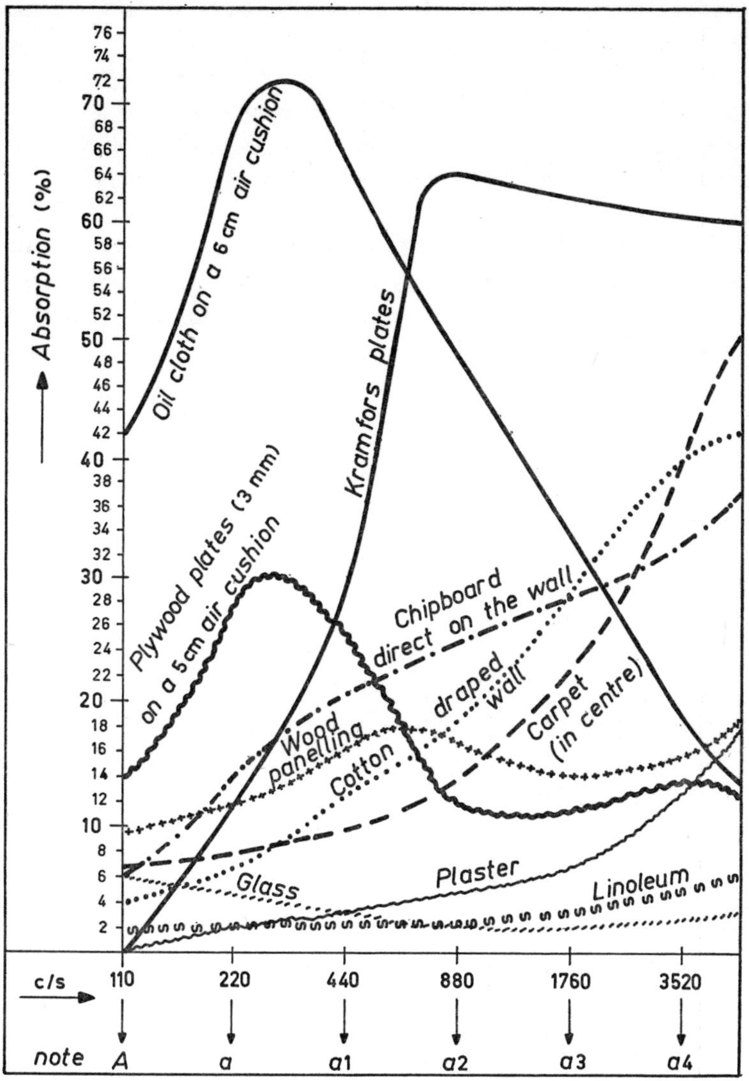

Fig. 1.6. Frequency dependency of the absorption of various materials

therefore, be as wrong to completely eliminate the reverberation of a room as it would be to maximise it. There are, for instance, basic differences between the acoustics of a hall where speeches are given, and a hall intended for musical performances [8].

For 'speech' the increase in volume caused by indirect sound is desirable, but not reverberation which has a deteriorating effect on 'intelligibility'. Indirect sound received 50 msec later than direct sound has a useful effect on the sound volume without directional impression and intelligibility being affected. But indirect sound delayed by more than 50 msec reduces intelligibility. For in that case the successive speech sounds begin to mask each other. In theatres and lecture halls indirect sound delayed by less than 50 msec is, if possible, aimed directly at the audience, while sounds delayed more than 50 msec are greatly suppressed.

For music, both diffusion and reverberation form important ingredients in the beauty of sound. To do full justice to a symphony orchestra, for instance, a large hall and reverberation times between 1.8 and 2.5 sec are required. A church organ requires a still larger hall and even longer reverberation times.

The reverberation time has been found to be a most important criterion in designing and assessing rooms and halls [1], although this criterion alone is not sufficient to characterise a room completely. A bathroom and the nave of a church can, for instance, have equal reverberation times. Still the acoustic impressions given by the two are entirely different. Technicians will be mainly interested in the electrical control of the acoustics of rooms and halls. This technique is based on certain acoustic effects in closed rooms, which can be summarised in the following three points [8].

1. There is a basic difference between *direct* and *indirect* sound. Direct sound gives a stereophonic impression of what is happening on the stage or in the orchestra. It more or less 'defines' sound.
   By means of sound colour, diffusion and reverberation, indirect sound gives an impression of the type of room and its volume. It gives sound 'dimensions' and makes music rich in tone. The more sound is diffused, the more pronounced these effects will be. The intelligibility of speech is reduced by sound which is delayed more than 50 msec.

2. The delay of 'indirect' sound tells us something about the size of the room.
3. The intensity 'ratio' between 'direct' and 'indirect' sound is decisive for distance perception.

The intelligibility of speech in a room can be tested by determining to what extent listeners can hear meaningless standardised syllables pronounced by a speaker. The percentage of syllables which are clearly understood stands for the syllable intelligibility. Fig. 1.7 shows the relation between syllable intelligibility and frequency range. In Fig. 1.8 intelligibility is plotted against reverberation time [7]. Intelligibity also depends on the width of the reproduced frequency band. The curve drawn in Fig. 1.7 shows limit values for the high and low frequencies respectively. It is clear that low frequencies can be substantially suppressed without noticeably affecting intelligibility.

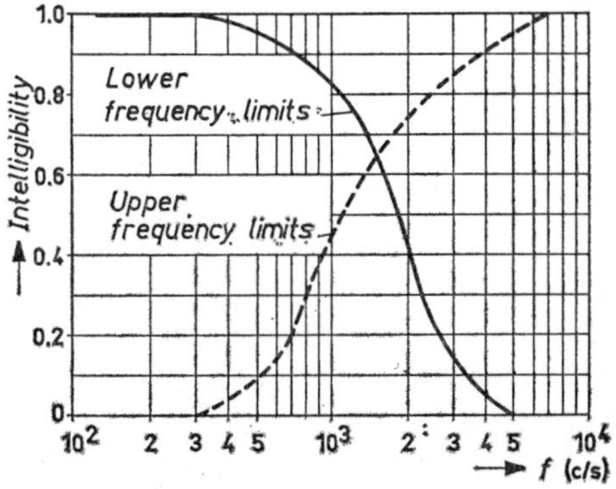

Fig. 1.7. Relation between syllable intelligibility and frequency range

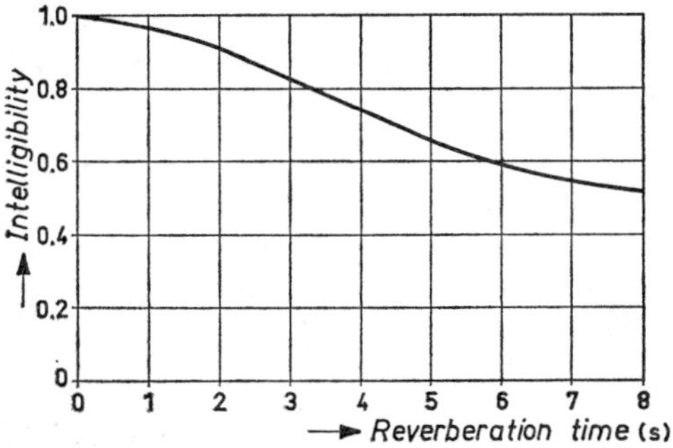

Fig. 1.8. Relation between syllable intelligibility and reverberation

The ear certainly perceives a deterioration of musical quality however, if the frequency band is narrowed as shown in Fig. 1.9. This proves that the low frequencies are important for judging the 'quality' of sound. According to a general rule the product of the upper and lower frequency limits must be 400,000 c/s to obtain maximum 'musicality'.

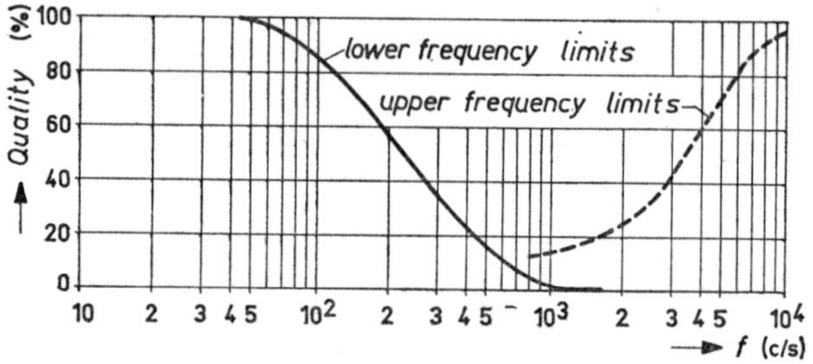

Fig. 1.9. Effect of upper and lower frequency limitation on quality

This leads to the conclusion that there are striking differences between the desirable acoustics of speech halls and of halls intended for musical performances. Fig. 1.10 clearly shows what the effect of a long reverberation time are on intelligibility, and it also indicates an electro acoustical method for suppressing undesirable effects. Fig. 1.10a shows that a speaker in a large hall with a long reverberation time can still be clearly heard on the front rows. Farther to the rear, however, intelligibility is impeded by too much indirect sound (compare the curves showing the intensities of direct sound I_d and indirect sound I_{ind} as functions of the distance to the speaker). Finally Fig. 1.10b shows that the speaker can be made quite intelligible in every row if a group of loudspeakers are employed to focus the sound at the rear half of the hall, making I_d become large compared with I_{ind} in all places [8].

In the same way the opposite effect can of course, be achieved if, for example, a room with a short reverberation time must be adapted for musical performances. The problem is then solved by means of 'ambiophony' (sometimes called stereo reverberation) [1, 8]. An example is given in Fig. 1.11. For the sake of clarity only one microphone (M) in front of the orchestra is shown. The microphone signal is magnetically recorded on the circumference of a rotating wheel (W) via recording head (0). The rotating wheel is called 'delay wheel'. Once having been recorded, the signal successively

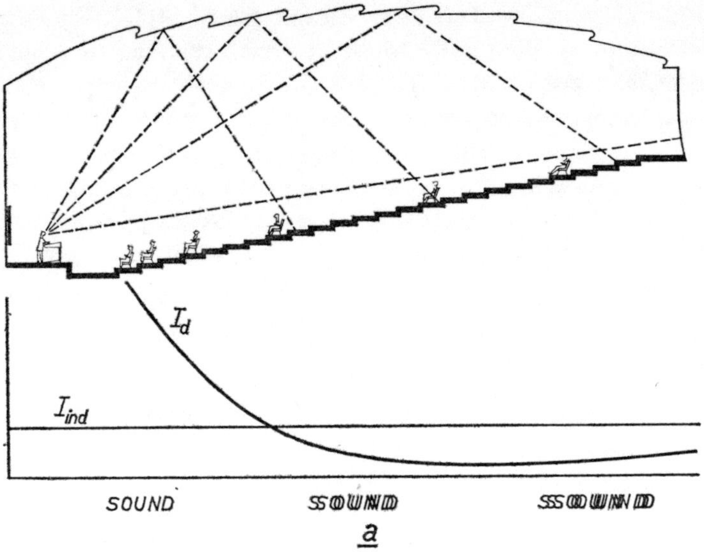

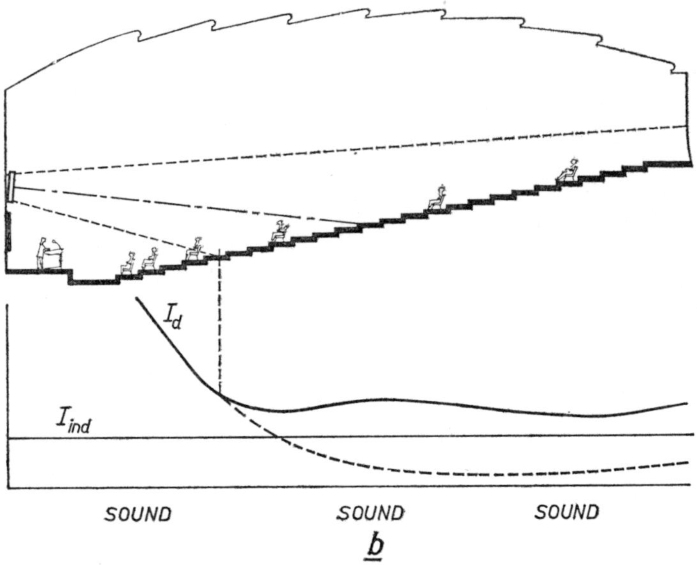

Fig. 1.10. Effects of the reverberation times on intelligibility. In a large hall with a long reverberation time a speaker can be distinctly heard in the first rows (a). If, by means of a loudspeaker column the sound is directed to the rear of the hall, the speaker can be clearly heard everywhere in the hall (b)

passes four play-back heads (1 — 4) and an erasing head (5). The latter ensures that all sections (*m*) of the wheel are demagnetised before again arriving under the recording head (*O*). The signals produced in the play-back heads are delayed with respect to the microphone signal, the delay times depending on the distance between the record head and each play-back head as well as on the speed at which the wheel rotates. Each play-back head drives via individual amplifiers (A_1 — A_4), its own group of loudspeakers specially arranged in the hall for the production of 'diffuse' sound. Consequently the loudspeakers must be so mounted that a minimal proportion of the sound they produce is projected directly towards the public. Each of

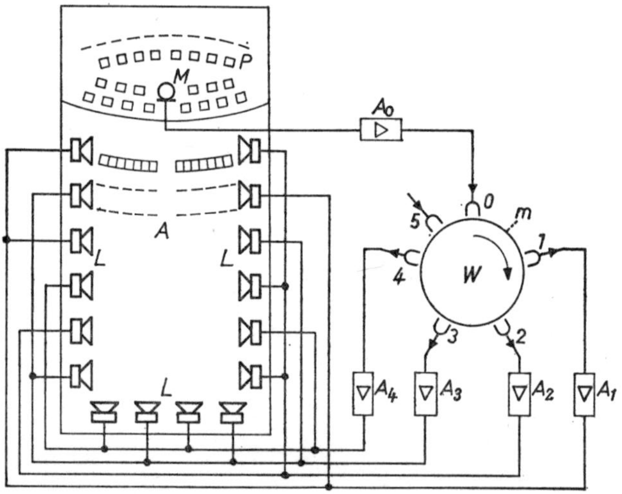

Fig. 1.11. Principle of an ambiophony installation. With this installation a room with a short reverberation time can be adapted for musical performances

these groups is given the correct intensity, tone colour and delay, and electrical feedback between the play-back heads and the recording head can also be used in order that the required results are ultimately obtained. The 'diffuse' and 'delayed' sound thus obtained supplements the insufficient quality of 'indirect' sound produced by the walls of the room. The major part of the sound may quite well come from the loudspeakers without the audience noticing. The arrangement of such an installation is, however, most critical. Exaggeration spoils the natural sound impression and betrays the presence of the installation. On the other hand, with perfect arrangement and adjustment of the installation, a performance really stands to gain by ambiophony. Ambiophony installations can also be used to make rooms seem more spacious or to create the illusion of concert-hall acoustics for open-air performances.

1.3 Monophonic or stereophonic reproduction?

It may seem strange that this section bears the heading 'Monophonic or stereophonic reproduction?' Yet this is the vital question technicians constantly have to answer as stereophony marches on, and which outsiders are always asking them.

The answer should not simply be given in favour of stereophonic reproduction without further consideration, although stereophony is undeniably a step forward on the way to perfect sound reproduction At any rate an objective view should be taken with regard to the main purpose. Assuming for a moment that it would be absolutely useless to reproduce words spoken from one point, the lectern, stereophonically, quite a number of people would also be content with a seat in the back row in a concert hall. Why should they? Some of them would not be able to notice any difference between quality in the front seats and that in the back row. Even the most enthusiastic efforts to interest such people in stereophony are doomed from the outset. On the other hand, stereophonic reproduction is out of place where perhaps functional music is the main purpose.

Apart from radio plays, the possibilities of stereophonic reproduction consist mainly of musical performances. Since it is a pleasure to listen to 'live' musical performances, it should also be possible to enjoy faithful reproductions of such performances! Here the answer is all in favour of stereophony provided, of course, that the three inseparable ingredients — stereo technique, Hi-Fi, and home studio technique are correctly employed. The reason for this close relationship is obvious. As the principal aim has always been to obtain faithful sound reproduction, development automatically led to stereo technique and Hi-Fi. The earlier 'monophonic' reproduction with ample 'diffuse' sound radiation was employed only because it was the only means available. Unfortunately so-called 'pseudo stereophonic effects' were used in combination with monophonic reproduction to give the public an impression of space. This had nothing whatsoever to do with stereophony.

But Hi-Fi developments also depended on the technical possibilities. Whereas in 1953 a frequency range from 40 to 15,000 c/s was regarded as 'suitable', and a range from 30 to 20,000 c/s as almost the extreme limit [14], in 1960 a range from 10 to 30,000 c/s was the 'least acceptable' and the frequency linearity even had to surpass the limit of audibility by at least one octave [15]. The same applies to other characteristics. Initially the human ear was used as a reference to compare the reproduction quality [14], a method long since abandoned.

Although a Hi-Fi installation can be adjusted to taste, several elements of the installation still have to meet certain requirements. It is a well-known fact that owing to distortion each element leaves its mark on the quality of the reproduction. Even under the best conditions only 'linear' distortion of the signal can be compensated by making special adjustments. There is no way, however, of eliminating inherent or resulting 'non-linear' distortion [15].

Alluding to a previous statement that reproduced music should provide as much pleasure as the original performance, one could hardly expect to get a good dinner in a wine cellar; neither should one expect to hear a symphony concert from a musical box. This implies (see Section 1.2), that music can best be enjoyed in suitable surroundings. In this respect two practically identical ideas were brought forward almost simultaneously. In Central Europe proposals were made [16] to transmit T.V. programmes with stereo sound as: 'in this case it can be taken for granted that apart from remaining in one place in the room, the viewer will be sufficiently attentive, which is a first requirement for a successful stereo programme. Radio stations could substantially enrich their programmes by means of TV concerts till then quite unjustifiably ignored.' On the other hand the news came from North America [17] that the F.C.C. (Federal Communications Commission) were considering stereo-multiplex for TV sound, and 'whether stereophonic sound contributed to reality', and if so, 'what kind of system should be used'. This seems to provide adequate proof that all this is not merely some arbitrary notion but where the actual realisation is concerned it is rather a positive contribution towards the faithful reproduction of musical performances.

Faithful or natural reproduction of music remains the principal aim of electro-acoustics, also in cases involving high frequency transmission. In the introduction to this chapter the expression 'hole-in-the-wall effect' or 'open window' was mentioned, which means that if only one loudspeaker is used one gets the impression of listening at an open window of a concert hall [10]. One can, however, vividly imagine the sigh of relief by latecomers to a concert when, after having heard the introduction, they finally enter the hall through a half opened door. This is a clear indication that there is something wrong with music produced by a voluminous sound source reaching the ear through a small opening. Stereophony is the only way of avoiding this open window or hole-in-the-wall effect.

Developments of stereophonic sound transmission were initially based on binaural sound perception. An explanation is given in Fig. 1.12. In room I a dummy head contains two microphones to imitate binaural hearing. The listener in room II hears the music played in room I via his headphones both connected to the two microphones in the dummy head; again binaural sound perception. The impression thus gained can already be highly realistic. If, however, the listener in room II slightly turns his head to one side or even backwards, he will still have the impression of looking in the direction of the sound source. This implies that his acoustical world seems to turn with him. The drawbacks of this method are obvious.

Thanks to the fact that our ears receiving sound from two loudspeakers mounted at some distance apart and connected to the microphones in the dummy head give the impression that we are listening to one apparent sound source seemingly located between the two actual sources, it became possible to achieve stereophonic reproduction of sound, see Fig. 1.13. In

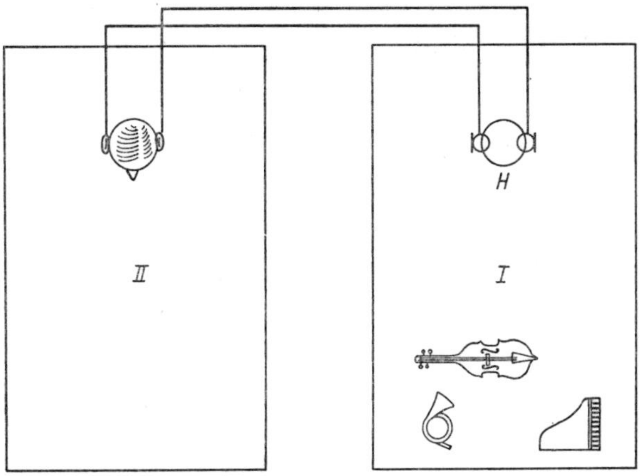

Fig. 1.12. Developments of stereophonic sound transmission were initially based on binaural sound perception. A dummy head fitted with two microphones 'listens' to the music played in room I. The observer in room II listens in room I via a set of headphones

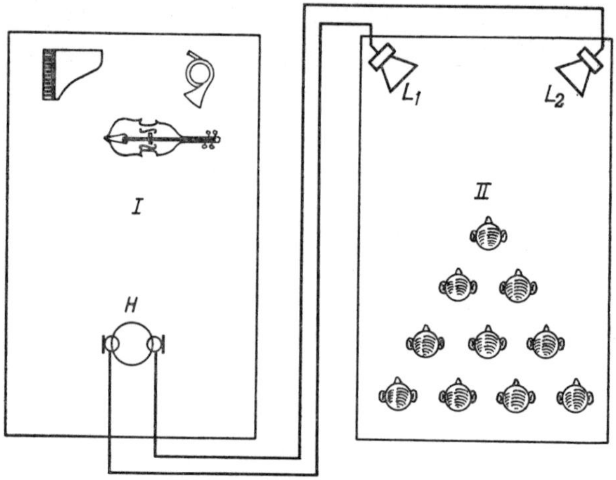

Fig. 1.13. Improved system shown in Fig. 1.12. The listener in room II gets the impression of space

contrast with Fig. 1.12 the microphones in the dummy head are connected to two loudspeakers instead of the headphones. In this way the audience in room II gets the impression of spaciousness.

So the answer to the question contained in the heading 'Monophonic or stereophonic sound reproduction?' should unanimously be in favour of stereophonic reproduction if the principal aim is 'natural' sound. In the following chapters it will be explained what methods are used.

CHAPTER 2

LF STEREOPHONY

The human ear can only recognise sound vibrations in the low frequency range. Sound recording, storing, and reproduction are therefore concerned only with these low frequencies (LF). It would therefore seem reasonable to discuss these processes first before considering HF stereophony which is more or less a branch of the radio transmission of LF stereophony.

2.1 Recording

Recording consists in capturing sound, for example by means of microphones, in order to store it for reproduction at some later time. The great variety of musical instruments produce between them sounds covering a considerable range of frequencies. Fig. 2.1 indicates the range of fundamental frequencies covered by each separate instrument [13]. The lowest fundamental note is produced on an organ: C2 which has a frequency of 16.35 c/s. The lowest note on the piano is A2 with a frequency of 27.5 c/s. The highest note on the piano is C5, 4,168 c/s. The organ also produces the highest note of all musical instruments. The sound spectrum of any instrument, however, is in fact much wider, since it includes the various harmonics.

The human ear cannot always register such frequencies. The hearing range of the human ear falls off towards higher notes. Table 2.1 gives figures which are the results of measurements involving 70 test persons [13].

The tests were carried out with a sound intensity of 60 phon, which corresponds with normal loudspeaker reproduction (see Table 1.1). Although the number of test persons may seem low, the values of Table 2.1 are still enlightening, for already it shows that notes of frequencies of 16 kc/s and more are not recognised by a large percentage of adults. It should, however, be borne in mind that according to the latest investigations the highest notes, even if they are not heard as such, have a definite effect on the total sound impression.

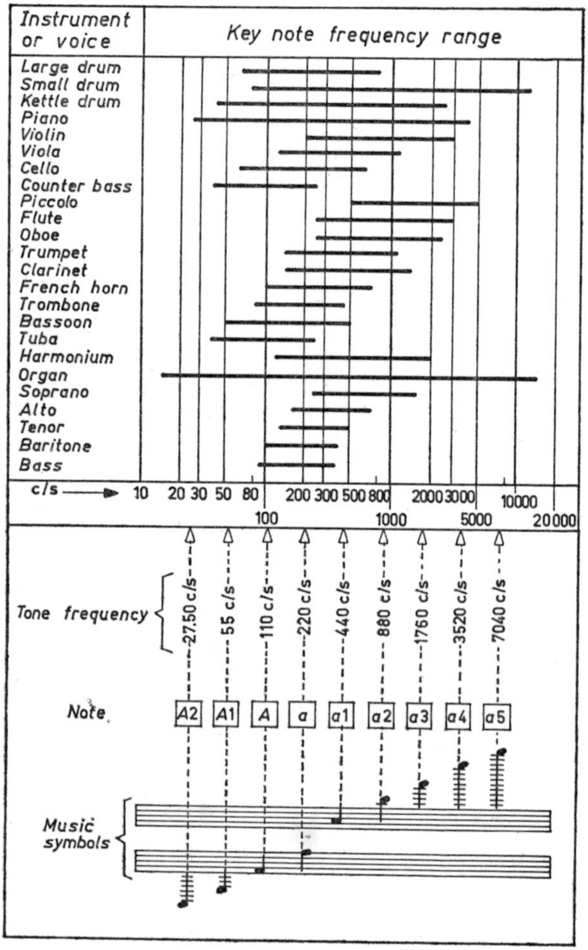

Fig. 2.1. Frequency range of the fundamental notes of various instruments and voices

TABLE 2.1

The following number could perceive sound up to a frequency of	out of every ten persons in the ages between						
	5-9 years	10-19 years	20-29 years	30-39 years	40-49 years	50-59 years	60-69 years
16,000 c/s*)	10	9	6	3	1	0	0
15,000	10	9	8	5	2	1	0
14,000	10	10	9	6	3	1	0
13,000	10	10	10	7	4	2	1
12,000	10	10	10	8	6	3	2
11,000	10	10	10	10	7	5	3
10,000	10	10	10	10	8	7	6
9,000	10	10	10	10	10	9	8
8,000	10	10	10	10	10	10	9

*) at a sound intensity of 60 phon

In sound recording the frequency range alone is not the decisive factor, for the sound level too, plays an important part. The human ear perceives sound intensities between 0 and 130 phon (see Table 1.1). In musical programmes this range of intensities is, of course, not fully used. After all the function of music is not to strain the ear to the threshold of feeling. Even so, volume, and to a certain extent the differences in sound levels which in live performances given by large symphony orchestras can assume a ratio between pianissimo and fortissimo of 1 : 1000, cannot be transmitted by electro acoustical means. Neither would that be desirable, for if it were possible, a radio set producing piano music which is just audible would burst out of its cabinet at the next fortissimo. Therefore, in order to avoid the piano sound from being drowned by unvoidable interference noise, a volume ratio of about 1 : 100 is used in radio transmission, which corresponds to about 40 dB [6]. This does not mean that now the electro acoustical limit as regards sound level has been reached. On the contrary, this example serves to illustrate that it is impossible to introduce the total volume range of a concert hall into the livingroom. This no longer has anything to do with the enjoyment of music as mentioned in Section 1.3.

After having more or less outlined the frequency and volume range of audible events, let us now consider how they are recorded *). Roughly speaking there are two types of audible events: one which is actual sound, while the other is available in the form of an electric signal. The latter

*) The recording of any work of music or literature protected by copyright is prohibited unless prior permission has been obtained from the author or his representatives.

category includes, for instance, radio programmes which, after demodulation, are recorded as LF signals. Furthermore, there are telephone conversations recorded on a so-called telephone adapter, and any other kind of reproduction from records or tapes. In each of these cases a microphone was used to record the sound event.

The microphone can be regarded as a device for converting sound into an LF electrical signal. Exactly the opposite takes place in loudspeakers where the electrical signal is converted again into audible sound. Microphones are divided into pressure microphones and pressure gradient microphones. There are also combinations of both principles. Microphones also differ as to their directional characteristics. Fig. 2.2 gives a survey of the most usual types of microphones and their corresponding characteristics. The directional characteristic in Fig. 2.2a has the form of a circle or a sphere; the microphone is equally sensitive in all directions. The diagrams shown in Fig. 2.2b, c and d differ from the circular characteristic. They are the figure of eight-shaped characteristic (Fig. 2.2b) of a bilaterally sensitive microphone, the cardioid-shaped (Fig. 2.2c) and hyper or super cardioid-shaped characteristic (Fig. 2.2d) of two unilaterally sensitive microphones. It should be noted that instead of 'cardioid-shaped' the expressions 'kidney-shaped' or 'heart-shaped' are often used.

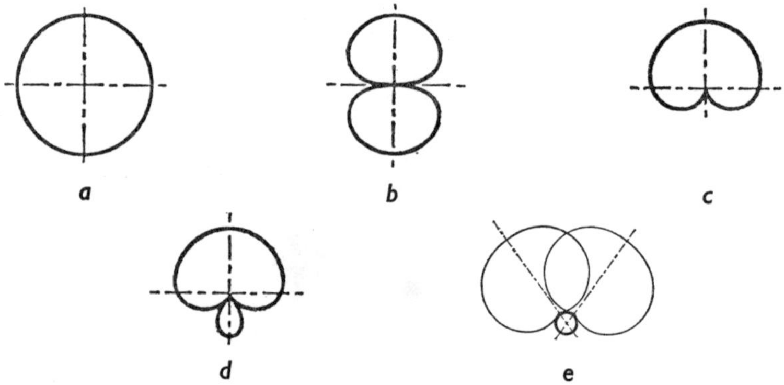

Fig. 2.2. Directional characteristics of various types of microphones; circular and sphere-shaped (a), figure-eight shaped (b), cardioid (c), hyper and super cardioid respectively (d), and the cardioid characteristic of a stereo microphone (e)

It will be clear that for stereo recordings stereo microphones are needed. Apart from the initially used dummy head representing a human head with two microphones built into the ears, and other special arrangements of microphones, wide use is made of stereo microphones which generally consist of one housing containing two microphones with cardioid characteristics, mounted one on top of the other and so arranged that the directions of highest sensitivity form an angle of 90° (Fig. 2.2e). Table 2.2 gives a specification of the microphones described above [13]. Such specifications and data concerning sensitivity and impedance are given in descriptions of microphones. With stereo microphones it is important that the two channels are very similar. A difference of ≦ 3 dB between the electro-acoustic indices in the range from 250 to 8,000 c/s is permissible [4].

For obvious reasons the contact arrangement of plug-in devices for microphones have been standardised [18]. However, two types of plugs and corresponding sockets shown in Fig. 2.3 are used. Fig. 2.3a shows the so-called DIN-plug (according to DIN 41 524), while the other one, Fig. 2.3b, is an IEC in-line plug. Apart from form and dimensions there are differences in the contact arrangement. With the DIN plug the contact order is 1, 4, 2, 5, 3. This may seem somewhat strange. This plug, however, was preceded by a 3-pin version whose contacts were numbered 1, 2 and 3 corresponding with the contact positions 1, 2 and 3 of a 5-pin plug. The contacts 4 and 5

TABLE 2.2

Directional characteristic	Sensitivity	Principle	Construction	Compare figure
circular spherical	omni-directional	pressure microphone	carbon, crystal moving coil, ribbon and capacitor microphone	2.2a
figure-of-eight	bilateral	pressure gradient microphone	moving coil, ribbon and capacitor microphone	2.2b
cardioid (kidney) or heart-shaped	unilateral	pressure, pressure gradient microphone	crystal, moving coil, ribbon and capacitor microphone	2.2c
hyper and super cardioid	unilateral	pressure, pressure gradient microphone	crystal, moving coil, ribbon and capacitor microphone	2.2d
double cardioid	double unilateral at an angle of 90°	pressure, pressure gradient microphone	crystal, moving coil, ribbon and capacitor microphone	2.2e

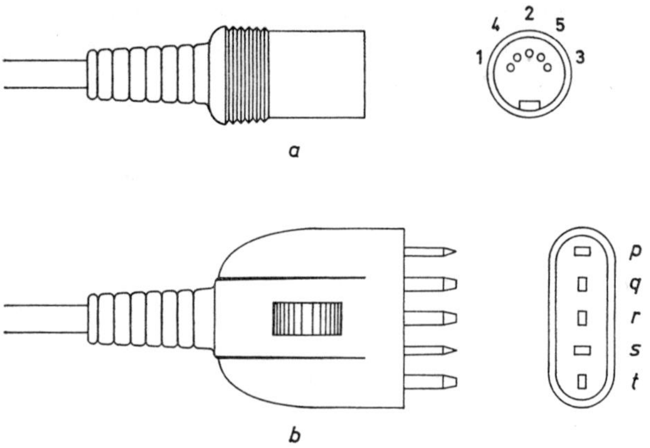

Fig. 2.3. The usual types of plug; DIN plug (a) and IEC in-line plug (b). The righthand side shows the arrangement of the pins

were inserted afterwards. On the other hand the pins of the IEC plugs are indicated as *p*, *q*, *r*, *s*, *t*. The relation between the two types of plugs are as follows:

DIN plug	1	4	2	5	3
IEC plug	*p*	*t*	*r*	*q*	*s*

Fig. 2.4 shows the contact arrangement of DIN microphone plugs. The Figs 2.4a up to and including 2.4e are circuit diagrams for microphones used for monophonic recording. Figs 2.4a and 2.4b show microphones with a low internal impedance (50 — 300 Ω, symmetrical) and (50 — 500 Ω, asymmetrical) respectively. Fig. 2.4c shows a microphone with a capacitive internal impedance (500 — 3,000 pF), while Fig. 2.4d shows a microphone of medium and high internal impedance respectively (500 — 5000 Ω and 25 — 150 kΩ). Compared with Figs 2.4b and d, Fig. 2.4e is a combination of the two — a microphone with high and low internal impedance (50 — 500 Ω, 25 — 150 kΩ). In stereophony, however, this gives rise to certain difficulties. As Section 2.3 will show, the contact arrangement must be made to match the play-back equipment, for instance in case stereo microphones are used directly with tape recorders. Fig. 2.4f shows the connection of a stereo microphone EL 3757. In contrast with Fig. 2.4b, terminal 3 is vacant since recording takes place via terminals 1 and 4, while playback is performed via the terminals 3 and 5 (cf. Fig. 2.31).

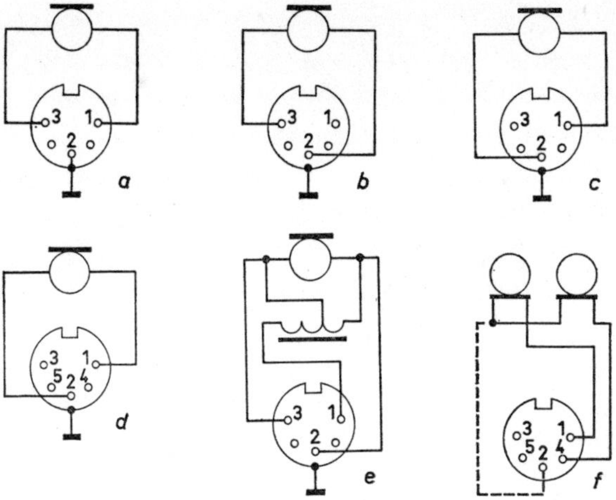

Fig. 2.4. Connections to DIN plugs as used for different types of microphones. An explanation is given in the text

The microphone arrangement presents an acoustical matching problem which can only be solved in the room concerned [8]. In so far as the microphones are used for sound recording or merely for the transmission of audible events, they can be mounted according to the usual studio method or purely empirically. It is a first requirement that mainly direct sound, and as little as possible reverberation and interfering sound, reaches the microphone, since interfering sounds are far more distinct in reproduction than when heard directly.

Conditions are quite different when the microphones are used for the transmission of sound in one and the same room. If the microphones pick up sounds from the loudspeakers, the result is acoustic feedback. This effect is strongest for frequencies in the sound spectrum for which the microphone shows a certain preference. As a result these notes are amplified to a greater extent than the others, and will continue longer. Such preference for certain notes and the resulting reverberation can be a real nuisance, immediately betraying the electro-acoustical nature of the sound, and having an unfavourable effect on the quality of the sound produced. These effects become more pronounced as amplification is increased, so that certain notes stand out more and more and begin to reverberate for a longer time. If amplification exceeds a certain limit, the installation begins to generate at the strongest preferred frequency. In practice the fault usually lies in wrong manipulation of the controls. Reverberation of certain notes is one of the principal complaints about sound installations, but in well designed installations it is a clear indication of excessive volume adjustment.

Acoustic feedback should be avoided at all costs. The problem becomes even more difficult due to the fact that the microphones must be inconspicuously mounted, or hidden altogether. This involves relatively large distances between microphones and sound source. The only solution then lies in the use of microphones with well defined directional properties. In this respect the applicability of a microphone finds its expression in the ratio between the sensitivity to the preferred direction (the directional sensitivity), and the sensitivity to all directions (the omni-directional sensitivity). For omni-directional microphones (see Fig. 2.2 and Table 2.2) with a circular characteristic this ratio is 0 dB; for microphones with figure-of-eight and cardioid characteristics about 5 dB, and for microphones with hyper and super-cardioid characteristics about 6 dB.

If there are no objections against the microphone arrangement from the visual point of view, the following values can be used as a guide [6]. Piano music is recorded with the instrument (piano or grand piano) open at the top, and the microphone located at a distance of about 50—75 cm from the right-hand side (descant side) of the instrument. String music is picked up at a distance of 0.5—1 m, and the same for woodwind instruments. For mouth organs a distance of 25—30 cm is used; for accordions, however, the distance should be 0.5—1 m. Brass instruments can be picked up at about 2 m. For drums and other percussion instruments the distance must be even greater. Singing can best be picked up at a distance of about 50 cm while the microphone should be mounted in an oblique position.

In many cases, in radio plays for instance, special sound effects are required. Such noises are mostly imitated by simple means in front of the microphone. Table 2.3 gives a few hints in this connection.

Further possibilities are the recording of radio programmes, copying gramophone records on magnetic tape, also tape-to-tape copying, and the 'taping' of telephone conversations. As already mentioned this section deals with recording in the widest sense of the word. In all examples given above a microphone recording has previously been made and only the LF signals recorded.

The recording of radio programmes and particularly stereo programmes on magnetic tape is fully justified only if reception of the programmes itself is sufficiently powerful. Exceptions should only be made for programmes

TABLE 2.3

Sound effect	Method
Crackling, blazing fire	Crumple a piece of cellophane or a plastic bag.
Ship's siren	Blow hard into a bottle neck.
Rifle shot	Strike the table with a flat ruler.
Thunder	Shake a large sheet of tin with both hands.
Crunching snow	Squeeze a bag of coarse meal with both hands.
Surf	Run a brush or broom over the parchment of a drum.
Roughly opened door	Strike a not too sturdy box, an orange box for instance, with a hammer.
Tearing shirt or trousers	Tear a piece of cloth.
Horse's hooves	Tap a hard surface with a coconut shell or a table tennis ball in each hand.
Rain	Sprinkle fine sand on a drum or shake peas steadily in a sieve.
Closing car door	Close a large tin with a bang.

which are of real historical interest. As with copying gramophone records or tape-to-tape copying, there are no points requiring special attention, none of these procedures require any professional skill with tape recorders. As stereophonic recording or 'taping' of telephone conversations, for which purpose a so-called telephone adapter is inductively coupled with the telephone is impossible in any case, it is only mentioned here in passing.

2.2 Sound carriers

From the very beginning of the art of sound recording, the gramophone record has always occupied an important place among sound carriers. Even in 1950 it was still considered the best means of conserving music. More recently, remarkable developments have taken place which, together with the magnetic tape, and of course also in a wider sense with FM radio transmission, render the gramophone record a source of high-quality LF sound. This has been reflected in the surging sales figures of the record industry. The repertoire now ranges from complete stereo recordings of operas, through jazz, entertainment music and popular hits to speech and noise records. The field of application seems almost boundless [19].

But how did this situation arise? The fact is all the more surprising as the end of the gramophone record had already been predicted on two occasions: first with the arrival of radio in the twenties, and again twenty-five years later, when the first amateur tape recorders came on the market [20]. A brief discussion of the technical development of the gramophone record might be of interest here.

For ages the wish to preserve fleeting sound has occupied scientists and inventors as well as charlatans. It took a long time before practical results were obtained. The 'Phonograph' patented in 1877 by Thomas A. Edison was the first practical system of mechanical sound recording. The sound carrier was a tin foil-coated roller with a helical sound groove. When reproducing the sound, a needle attached to a membrane and the well-known sound amplifying horn travelled through the groove, the rotating roller being moved axially by a guide screw. The movements made by the needle were analogous to the engraved audible events, and took place perpendicularly to the surface of the roller. This method of cutting sound grooves was called vertical or hill-and-dale recording. A great drawback of the phonograph roll was that it could not be mass-produced.

Ten years later Emil Berliner replaced the cylindrical sound carrier by a disc, and patented the first gramophone record. The sound grooves were now cut into a wax layer on zinc, and not perpendicular to but parallel with the surface; this process was called lateral recording. The recordings were fixed in an acid bath. Again it took years before a mass-producing method was developed. It was not until 1895 that the 'Berlin Gramophone Company' was established in Philadelphia. The first records brought on the market were made of hard rubber, were to be played on one side only and had a diameter of 17 cm!

Further developments brought the change from hard rubber to shellac as the sound carrier: the diameter increased to 25 and 30 cm, and the records could then be played on both sides. Other important milestones were electric recording, introduced in 1925; the electric pick-up and gramophone motor, appearing in 1930; light-weight pick-ups, and crystal pick-ups. The introduction of magnetic tape for sound recording, and in particular the change-over to long-playing records were also of great importance. The next steps Hi-Fi quality and the development of stereo gramophone records were the logical outcome.

The principles of modern stereo records are, therefore, not completely new; as early as 1931 an Englishman, A. D. Blümlein, patented a method of recording both the stereo signals in one groove. The system was a combination of vertical and lateral recording. The fact that development of the stereo record was not initiated before 1955 was due to the former imperfections involved in record production. Blümlein's method too, has undergone substantial improvements. The combination of vertical and lateral recording is no longer used; instead each of the two directions of movement is now at an angle of 45° with the surface of the record. This principle is illustrated in Fig. 2.5. The cutter is driven by signals fed to coils *L* and *R*. Consequently the directions of modulation are perpendicular to the inner and outer walls of the sound groove respectively. At the same time the left and right recordings are of equal quality, and each contains both lateral and vertical information. Only in this way can it be explained why a monophonic record produces sound via both channels when played back on a stereo installation. To some extent the record can then be regarded as a stereo record whose two channels are similarly modulated, that is to say, with only a lateral signal.

On the other hand it should also be possible to play a stereo record on a monophonic installation provided the record is 'compatible'. In principle this is quite possible provided the mono record player is fitted with a modern light-weight tone arm. As the pick-up of such an installation will only give horizontal but no vertical response, it is possible to reproduce only the lateral recording in the groove.

How lateral and vertical recording is combined can be briefly explained by means of Figs 2.6—2.11 [13]. If the left-hand coil system (*L* in Fig. 2.5) is energised, the cutter will move vertically with respect to the groove wall during recording (see Fig. 2.6). Consequently the modulation is only

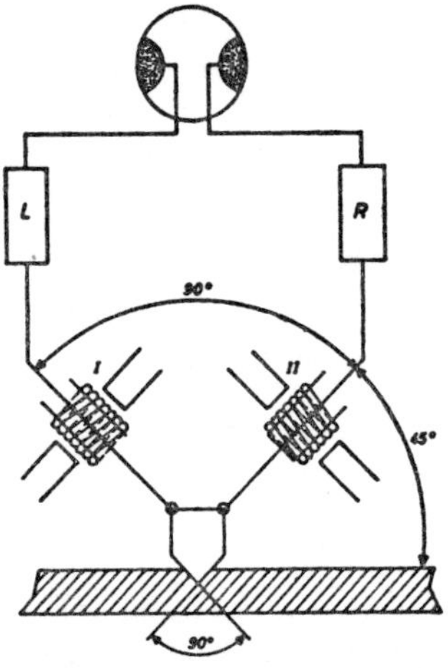

Fig. 2.5. Principle of stereo record cutting

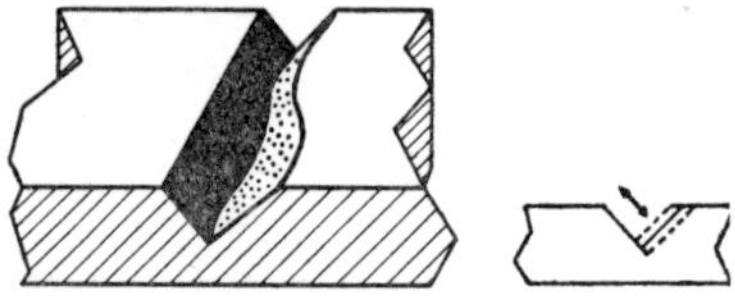

Fig. 2.6. Recording left-hand channel information

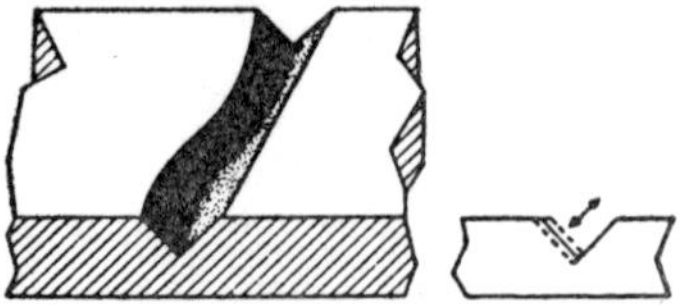

Fig. 2.7. Recording right-hand channel information

engraved into the right-hand wall of the groove, while the left-hand wall remains absolutely unmodulated. It can be clearly seen that the sound groove widens and narrows after modulation has taken place. As a result of this modulation the pick-up stylus will move not only laterally but also vertically. Fig. 2.7 shows a sound groove modulated only via the right-hand channel (*R* in Fig. 2.5). The result is a mirror reflection of Fig. 2.6 so that no further explanation is needed.

If both walls of the groove are modulated with signals of equal strength (see Fig. 2.8), while there is no phase (time) difference between the two signals, the cutter will move only up and down. The result is purely vertical recording; the sound groove widens and narrows alternately. How two forces can be combined to form one resulting force is explained by means of a practical example (see Fig. 2.9). If a boat is pulled with two ropes of equal length by two persons standing at the same distance from the boat, one on each bank of the river, the boat will move precisely along the centre line of the river. It also becomes clear from Fig. 2.9 what would happen if one of the two persons, for instance the one on the right, were to pull in the opposite direction (broken line); the boat would then move sideways towards the river bank.

In the same way it is possible to reverse the phase of one of the signals, e.g. the right-hand signal, electrically. If the requirements of Fig. 2.8 — equal

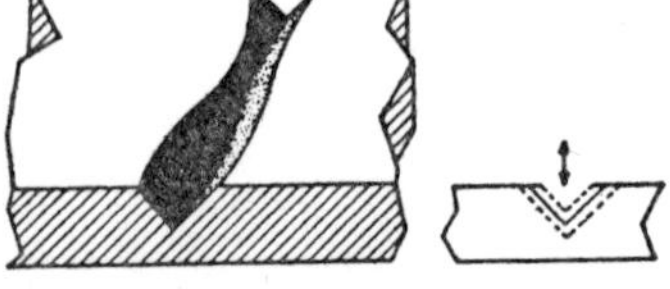

Fig. 2.8. Simultaneous recording of *L* and *R* information; no phase (time) difference between the two signals

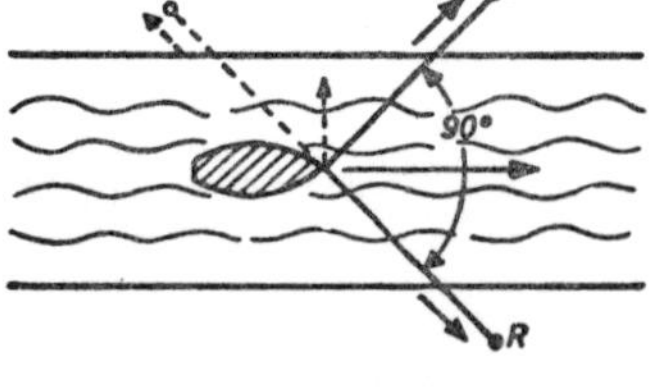

Fig. 2.9. How two forces combine to form one resulting force (the resultant) is explained by means of a practical example

intensity and phase of both channels — are satisfied, the reverse force exercised by the right-hand coil (*R* in Fig. 2.5) will give the cutter a purely lateral motion. The result is a laterally modulated sound groove as used for mono records (see Fig. 2.10).

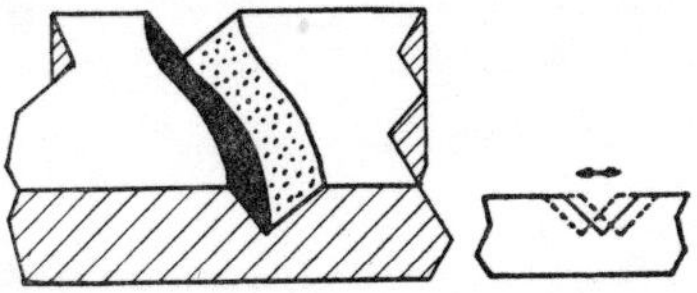

Fig. 2.10. A laterally modulated sound groove is obtained by reversing one of the coil systems (*R* in Fig. 2.5) if the requirements mentioned in Fig. 2.8 are satisfied

The situations explained by means of Figs 2.6, 2.7, 2.8 and 2.10 occur but relatively seldom in actual stereophonic recording. Generally the two signals show a difference both in phase and intensity. Consequently the cutter moves vertically and horizontally at the same time. This is shown by a widening of the sound groove (see Fig. 2.11); there is simultaneous vertical and lateral modulation. The geometrical dimensions of record grooves, also decisive for the dimensions of the stylus, have been standardised [11]. This is explained in the drawings of Fig. 2.12. Fig. 2.12a shows normal groove N 78, Fig. 2.12b microgroove M 45 and M 33 while Fig. 2.12c represents stereo grooves St 45 and St 33. Table 2.4 gives further particulars.

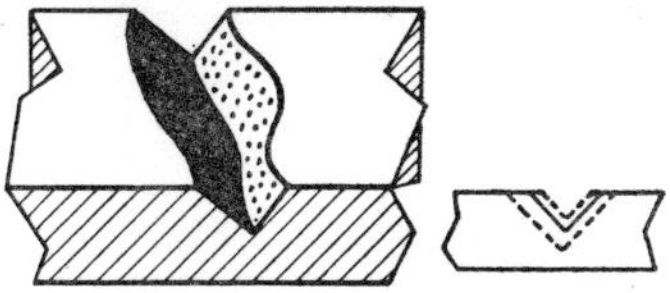

Fig. 2.11. Stereo sound groove with lateral and vertical modulation

TABLE 2.4

	Normal groove N 78	Microgroove M 45/M 33	Stereo groove St 45/St 33
Groove width	$\geqq$ 100 μm	$\geqq$ 55 μm	$\geqq$ 40 μm
Groove rounding	$\leqq$ 25 μm^r	$\leqq$ 4 μm^r	$\leqq$ 4 μm^r
Groove angle	88° ± 5°	90°	90°
Rounding of corresponding stylus	60 μm^r	12 . . . 25 μm^r	12 . . . 18 μm^r

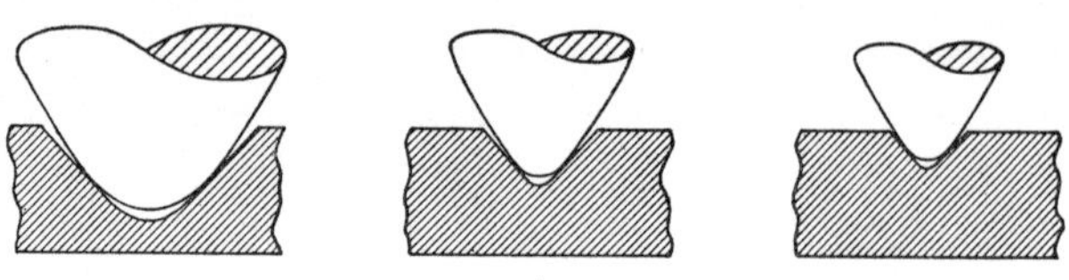

Fig. 2.12. The geometrical dimensions of the groove are also decisive for the dimensions of the stylus; normal groove N 78 (a), microgrooves M 45 and M 33 (b), stereo grooves St 45 and St 33 (c)

The stylus rests neither on the edges nor on the bottom of the groove [19]. The reason is that at too large a radius the stylus will be flung out of the groove while too small a radius may result in distorted sound reproduction as the stylus is not appropriately guided along the sound track. The stylus is in the ideal position when it touches the centre of the groove sides within the upper and lower tolerance limits. Fig. 2.13 shows different positions of the stylus. Figures 2.13a and 2.13b show the stylus resting on the edges and the bottom of the groove respectively; both positions should be avoided. The required position is that of Fig. 2.13c, where the stylus is in contact with the centres of the groove sides.

Thanks to exhaustive industrial tests and investigations the gramophone record still maintains its position among LF sound sources.

The recording of sound on discs is a purely mechanical process although the methods of record cutting and record playing are now electrically operated. Obviously this technique cannot be regarded as the last word in production methods. Although records can easily be turned out on a mass-production scale after a certain amount of preliminary work has been done, the production of a single record — especially for home use — is not a practicable proposition. Magnetic recording led to the development of magnetic tape as a sound carrier [22]. Little information was available during

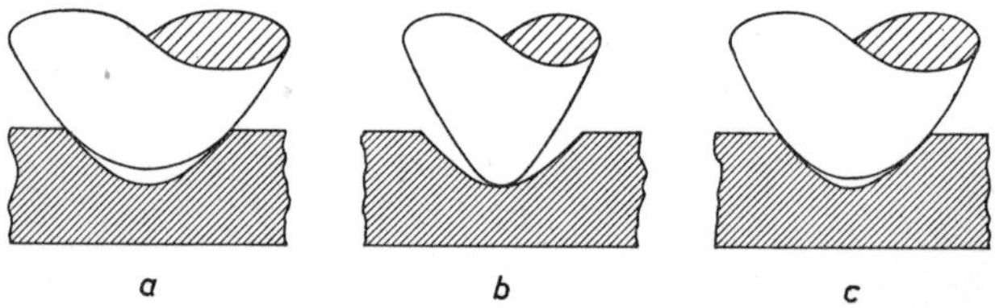

Fig. 2.13. Showing wrong positions (a and b), and correct position (c) of the stylus

the early days of this development, as those engaged in sound recording made use of gramophone records. The magnetic tape used to-day was preceded by steel tape and later by steel wire as the sound carrier. Steel tape and wire, however, did not possess the best magnetic characteristics for good sound reproduction so that they did not become very popular. The next step was the application of a cellulose tape carrying a layer of ferrous powder, which was indeed a great improvement. In 1940 this method underwent a basic change when von Braunmühl and Weber introduced the HF treatment of the sound carrier. Apart from later refinements sound recording then became what it still is to-day. The cellulose film as the basic material was in the meantime replaced by acetyl cellulose, polyvinyl chloride or polyester tapes on which the magnetic tape layer from 10 to 15 μm thick, was deposited. This layer is in fact a prepared iron oxide (Fe_2O_3 and Fe_3O_4).

Sound is recorded on the magnetic tape by varying the degree of magnetisation. For this purpose the tape is passed along an arrangement of recording heads at a constant speed. The principle is shown in Fig. 2.14. It should be mentioned here that there are also combinations of recording and playback heads, known as combined heads or 'combi-heads'. In early recordings the tape speed was 76 cm/sec. Consequently a tape 1,000 m long had a playing time of just 22 min.; multitrack techniques came later. Compared with tape speeds of 2.4 cm/sec and four-track recoıding, this seems an enormous waste. A summary of the usual tape speeds is given in Table 2.5.

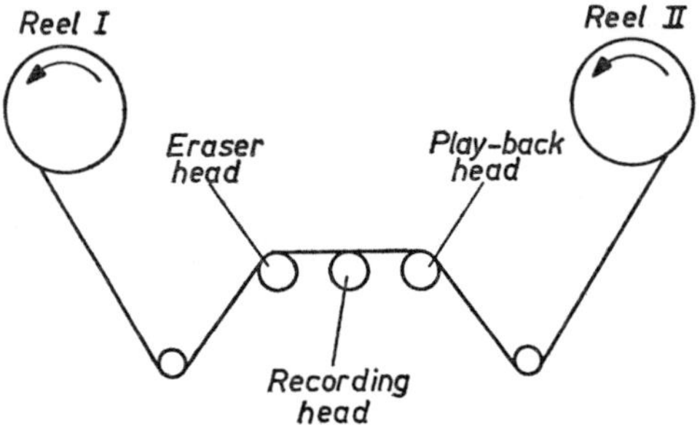

Fig. 2.14. Principle of head arrangement and tape transport on a tape recorder. Tape speeds of 45.6 and 18.3 cm/sec, and 17.95 and 7.2 inch/sec are used for film sound purposes

TABLE 2.5

cm/sec	76	45.6	38	19	18.3	9.5	4.75	2.4
inch/sec	30	17.95	15	7.5	7.2	3.75	1.875	0.94

Further developments and continued improvements of equipment made it possible to use ever lower tape speeds. Tape consumption finally became very economical so that tape recorders became attractive to amateur users also. For amateur use only speeds of 19, 9.5, 4.75 and 2.4 cm/sec (see table 2.5) are normally employed. Fig. 2.15 illustrates the tape transport for each of these four speeds.

Fig. 2.15. Comparison of the length of tape used per second for each of the four speeds

A tape speed of 9.5 cm/sec is the most popular for normal use [6]. It combines excellent reproduction qualities with economy. For still higher quality reproduction the more expensive types of recorders operate at tape speeds of 19 cm/sec. This speed is used mainly for Hi-Fi sound reproduction. Owing to the development of high quality micro heads, tape speeds of 4.75 cm/sec now give reasonably good quality reproduction also. This speed was formerly only used for speech and music recordings where high quality reproduction was not demanded. To-day, however, it provides recordings of a quality not so long ago obtainable only at speeds of 9.5 cm/sec, that is to say twice as fast. In view of this, a further 50% reduction of the tape speed seemed justified. This meant the acceptance of the 2.4 cm/sec speed giving still greater economy in use of the tape, particularly for speech recordings in which quality is of secondary importance.

The question now arises as to what is the best or most suitable tape speed. The answer is, of course, that each tape speed has its own advantages. The most suitable speed depends on the particular purpose, taking into consideration such factors as quality and tape consumption.

Initially the whole tape width (6.25 mm) was required for recording — the so-called 'single track' recording. The result of halving the width of this single track was the 'double track' whereby two adjacent recording tracks could be employed on one side of the tape. By halving each of the two halves again, the four-track tape came into use, which meant that one side of the tape accommodated four sound tracks. The saving in tape is indicated in Fig. 2.16 [13]. Fig. 2.16a shows a single track, Fig. 2.16b a double track and Fig. 2.16c a four-track tape.

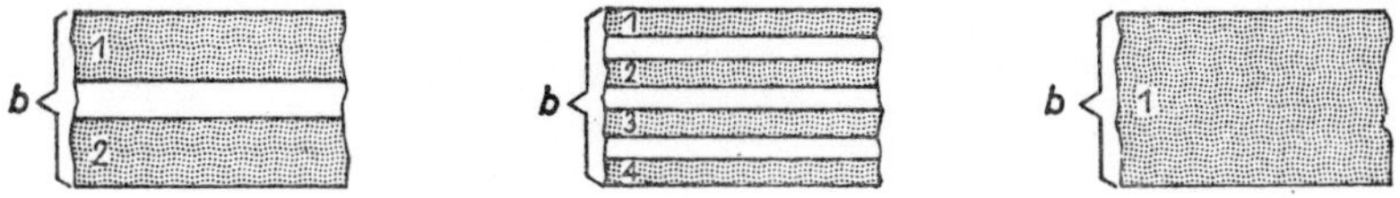

Fig. 2.16. Saving in tape achieved by double track halving; single track (a), double track (b), four-track (c) recording

It should be borne in mind that this saving involves a narrowing of the track width each time halving takes place. Whereas with 'single track' the whole tape width (6.25 mm) could be used, with double track there is hardly 3 mm left for each track. For four-track recording the track width is reduced to no more than 1 mm, as a certain amount of space is required between the individual tracks. The volume and noise distance thus diminished with the track width, so that appropriate measures, such as increasing the gain, lowering the interference level etc. were called for.

Fig. 2.17 shows the track arrangement on a double and four-track tape respectively. For double-track monophonic recordings tracks 1 and 2 are used in opposite directions of the tape. The same system is applied in four-track recording: first track 1 is used, then, when the tape is reversed, track 4. Only then (after second reversal of the tape) track 3 is used, and finally (third reversal of the tape) track 2. For stereo recording the playing time is, of course, reduced by 50%. In this case track 1 and track 2 are used for the left-hand and right-hand channels respectively on a double-track tape. With four-track recording track 1 is used for the left-hand channel and track 3 for the right-hand channel. After reversal of the tape, track 4 is used for the left-hand channel and track 2 for the right-hand channel. The beginning and end of tapes for domestic use are marked with a green and red strip respectively [23]. The back of the tape usually carries the name of the manufacturer, type indication and code number.

Recordings by double track apparatus can readily be played back on four-track equipment. Conversely four-track tapes can also be played on double-track apparatus. Herein lies the reason why on four-track sound tapes the sequential order is not 1, 2, 3 and 4 (mono) and $^1/_2$, $^3/_4$ (stereo), but 1, 4, 3, 2 (mono) and $^1/_3$, $^4/_2$ (stereo). Another reason is that the internal component of recording and play-back heads cannot be reduced in size indefinitely. Another reason for the special track arrangement is that one track runs free through the air gaps between the two sets of four-track heads (see Fig. 2.17).

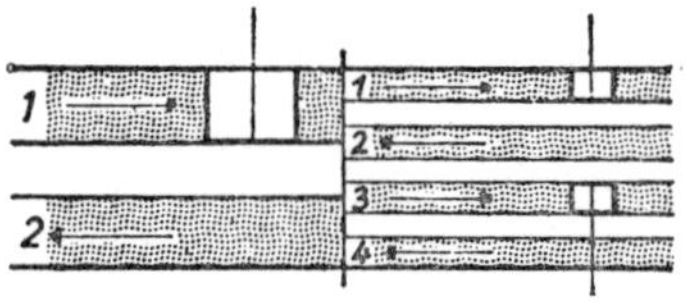

Fig. 2.17. Track arrangement on a double track and on a four-track tape

Table 2.6 gives a clear summary of the playing times of Philips sound tapes at various speeds both for double and four-track recordings. The indications refer to mono operation and should be divided by two for stereo operation.

Apart from gramophone records and sound tapes there are, of course, other sound carriers. For instance — mainly in use for sound pictures — there is the light sound system, in which the film itself is the sound carrier. For domestic sound-motion pictures the film strip incorporates a magnetic layer. The procedure is then the same as for sound tape.

Another important system is the Philips-Miller method which even before the arrival of the sound tape gave amazingly good sound recordings, with frequency response curves flat within ± 2 dB over a frequency range of 30—8000 c/s and relatively long recording times being obtained. Recording times of 10 minutes and even 30 minutes on special apparatus are possible. The sound carrier is a film strip known as the Philimil strip. This strip carries a layer of transparent gelatine about 60 μm thick overlaid by a thin opaque film about 3 μm thick. In sound recording a wedge-shaped cutter (see Fig. 2.18) scribes a transparent sound track — on an opaque underlayer — into the gelatine film. The Philimil tape is run at a speed of 45.6 cm/sec (standard film speed). The sound track is scanned by means of an optical system and a photocell. Reproduction can take place immediately after recording, which is a most welcome feature in many applications.

In view of the different types of sound carriers and methods of recording audible events, it is obvious that the characteristics of reproducers must also differ. It would, however, be beyond the scope of this book to give a full

TABLE 2.6

	Type	Reel dia.	Tape length	at 2.4 cm/sec 2-track	4-track	at 4.75 cm/sec 2-track	4-track
	PL 13	13 cm	270 m	2× 3 h	4× 3 h	2×1.5 h	4×1.5 h
1)	PL 15	15 cm	360 m	2× 4 h	4× 4 h	2× 2 h	4× 2 h
	PL 18	18 cm	540 m	2× 6 h	4× 6 h	2× 3 h	4× 3 h
	PD 8	8 cm	90 m	2× 1 h	4× 1 h	2× 30 min.	4× 30 min.
	PD 10	10 cm	180 m	2× 2 h	4× 2 h	2× 1 h	4× 1 h
2)	PD 13	13 cm	360 m	2× 4 h	4× 4 h	2× 2 h	4× 2 h
	PD 15	15 cm	540 m	2× 6 h	4× 6 h	2× 3 h	4× 3 h
	PD 18	18 cm	730 m	2× 8 h	4× 8 h	2× 4 h	4× 4 h
	PT 8	8 cm	135 m	2×1.5 h	4×1.5 h	2× 45 min.	4× 45 min.
3)	PT 10	10 cm	270 m	2× 3 h	4× 3 h	2×1.5 h	4×1.5 h

	Type	Reel dia.	Tape length	at 9.5 cm/sec 2-track	4-track	at 19 cm/sec 2-track	4-track
	PL 13	13 cm	270 m	2× 45 min.	4× 45 min.	2× 22 min.	4× 22 min.
1)	PL 15	15 cm	360 m	2× 1 h	4× 1 h	2× 30 min.	4× 30 min.
	PL 18	18 cm	540 m	2×1.5 h	4×1.5 h	2× 45 min.	4× 45 min.
	PD 8	8 cm	90 m	2× 15 min.	4× 15 min.	2× 7 min.	4× 7 min.
	PD 10	10 cm	180 m	2× 30 min.	4× 30 min.	2× 15 min.	4× 15 min.
2)	PD 13	13 cm	360 m	2× 1 h	4× 1 h	2× 30 min.	4× 30 min.
	PD 15	15 cm	540 m	2×1.5 h	4×1.5 h	2× 45 min.	4× 45 min.
	PD 18	18 cm	730 m	2× 2 h	4× 2 h	2× 1 h	4× 1 h
	PT 8	8 cm	135 m	2× 22 min.	4× 22 min.	2× 11 min.	4× 21 min.
3)	PT 10	10 cm	270 m	2× 45 min.	4× 45 min.	2× 22 min.	4× 22 min.

1) LP tape 2) double tape 3) triple tape

explanation of the principles of operation of a record player which are in any case well known. Moreover, there is specialised literature on the operating principles and applications of tape recorders [6, 22, 24]. As for each

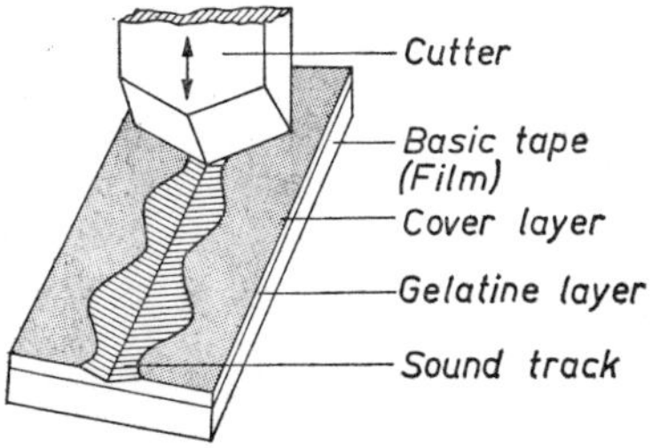

Fig. 2.18. Principle of Philips-Miller recording system

kind of reproduction an amplifier and loudspeaker are required, this section will deal with mainly these subjects.

2.3 Reproduction

A few preliminary remarks on sound reproduction from gramophone records will, however, not be out of place. Since the preceding chapter gave a description of how *L* and *R* information is recorded in one sound groove, it may be of interest to learn how these recordings are reconverted into sound. This is done by the pick-up head on which the quality of the reproduction mainly depends.

The operating principle of a stereo pick-up head is shown in Fig. 2.19. The stylus is connected to two crystals which are capable of being distorted. At their ends the crystals are interconnected by means of a W-shaped elastic coupling piece. The stylus arm drives the coupling piece at the centre. The front support (indicated) is made of flexible plastic, and the rear support is of rigid plastic, distortion is thus permitted to take place [13]. If, for instance, the right-hand wall of the groove is modulated, the stylus arm will begin to move perpendicularly to this wall. The same movements are made by the coupling piece. As a result only the right-hand system is distorted and supplies a voltage corresponding to the modulation (see Fig. 2.20a). The function of the left-hand groove wall can be explained in the same way, the only

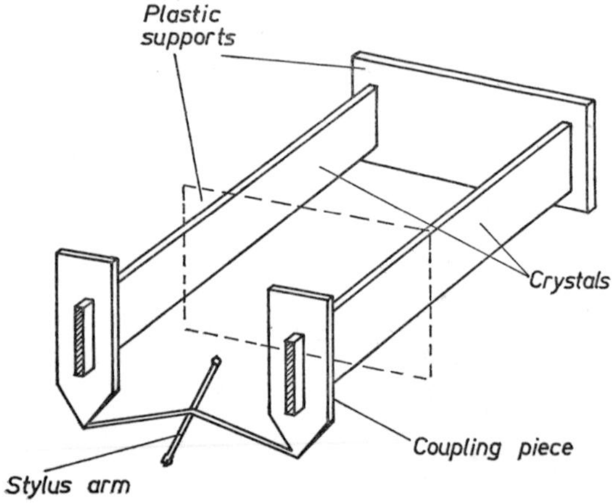

Fig. 2.19. Operating principle of a stereo pick-up head

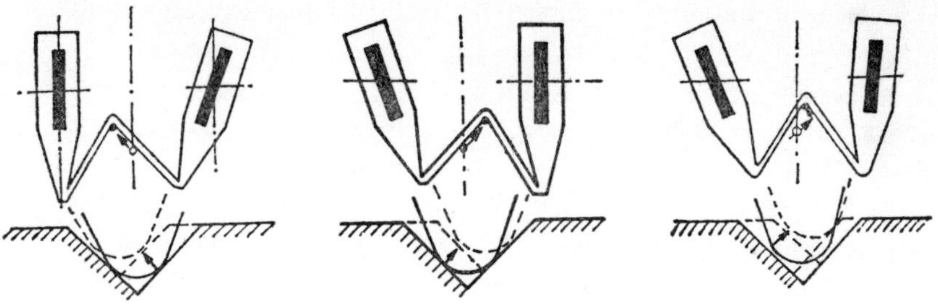

a b c

Fig. 2.20. Influence of the modulation of the right-hand wall (a), the left-hand wall (b) and both walls of the groove (c) on the system of the pick-up head

difference being that now the left-hand system is distorted (see Fig. 2.20b). In Fig. 2.20c, both walls of the groove are modulated at the same time. This causes distortion of both systems in the pick-up head. The information recorded in the two grooves is separated in the pick-up head and converted into two electric voltages. Fig. 2.21 gives an impression of the construction of a pick-up head.

As already stated in Section 2.2, not only are there specified dimensions for the width and rounding of the various grooves, but a certain rounding of the corresponding stylus (table 2.4) is also specified. Consequently indi-

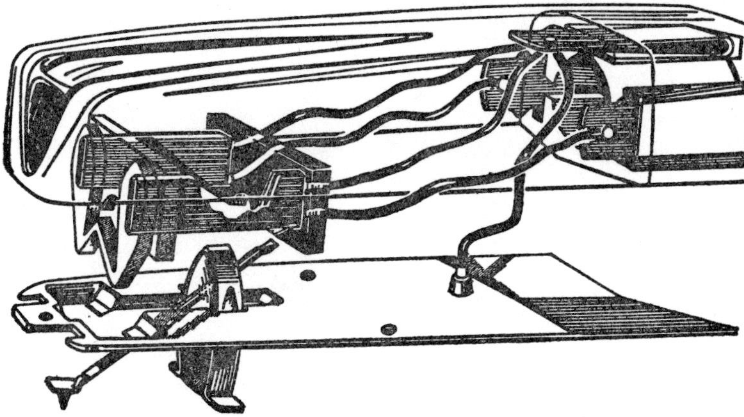

Fig. 2.21. Construction of a stereo pick-up head

vidual record players work at different stylus pressures which should be carefully checked. Moreover the construction of the driving mechanism plays an important part in the overall result. That is also the reason why for home studio technique (Hi-Fi), record players must satisfy minimum requirements [4].

Hi-Fi record player AG 2030 [25] is a good example of excellent design. Developments were aimed at producing a record player which would, at a reasonable cost, meet all the demands of Hi-Fi fans. The idea of incorporating automatic record changing was abandoned, since Hi-Fi lovers are not likely to use such apparatus. Furthermore, for reasons of sound quality the pick-up arm of Hi-Fi record players should not be loaded with the unavoidable operating components of a changer mechanism. For the same reason record player AG 2030 is not fitted with a mains switch operated by the pick-up arm. When the record is finished, the pick-up arm is merely lifted off the record. If required, the automatic lift can be put out of operation. The positioning mechanism for the pick-up arm is a valuable feature, greatly facilitating operation. By means of a lever the pick-up arm can be carefully lowered to, and raised from, any point on the record. The construction includes semi-automatic lifting of the pick-up arm by means of viscosity damping which functions independently of the drive mechanism and enables any number of positionings at any point on the record, including the immediate vicinity of the run-out groove.

Obviously such a record player is also fitted with a first class pick-up head, the AG 3407, for instance, operating on the magnetodynamic principle. The stylus carrier, fitted with a diamond stylus at the front, has a receptacle containing a fine ferroxcube rod at the end. There it is resiliently mounted between the pairs of poles of two induction coils, and can move in two planes, thus following all undulations in a stereo groove. Due to the movements of the stylus, and consequently the movements of the carrier with the magnetic rod, voltages are induced in the respective coils of the pole pairs.

The advantage of this system lies in the rigid connection between stylus and magnet, which is established by the stylus carrier, and also in the exceedingly low inertia of the moving system. As the signal (and this applies to all dynamic pick-up heads) must be amplified and simultaneously adapted to the frequency range of the record, the record player can be equipped with a transistorised pre-amplifier AG 9021. The frequency response curve of the pick-up head is practically level between 20 c/s and 20 kc/s, and within 2.5 dB. Fig. 2.22 gives the resonance-free frequency response curve of a

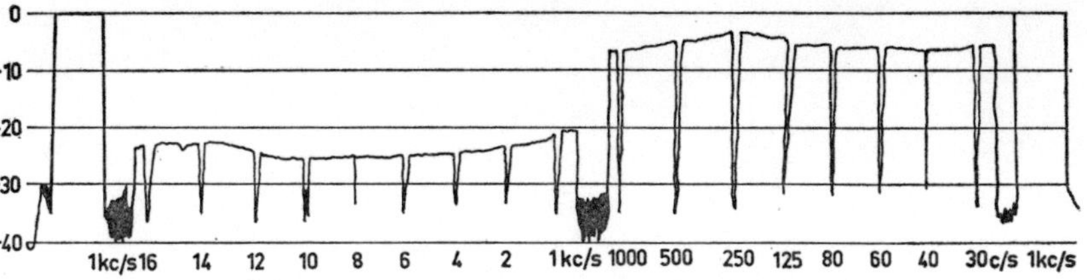

Fig. 2.22. Frequency range of a pick-up head AG 3407

pick-up head AG 3407 and pre-amplifier AG 9021 for the total audio range. It should be noted that each pick-up head AG 3407 carries a mark indicating its frequency response.

Record players and also tape recorders supply signals to amplifiers and loudspeakers. Tape recorders have an exceptionally wide field of application [22, 24]. Thanks to a whole range of accessories they can be used for a large variety of purposes [26]. Examples are, for instance, automatic slide projection, remote control, foot switches, telephone adapters, headphones etc. For home studio tape recorders too (Hi-Fi), there are certain minimum requirements as regards the respective applications [4]. As the introduction of this chapter already suggests, the main stress will be laid on amplifiers and loudspeakers, as these are indispensable items for all systems of sound reproduction.

At the beginning of Chapter I mention was made of the paths which had been trodden before stereophony could be introduced on a wide basis, in order to achieve sound reproduction of the highest possible quality in living rooms [3]. Every effort was made to eliminate the so-called 'hole-in-the-wall' or 'open window' effect, by diffusing the sound (see Fig. 1.1).

Something about frequency ranges in which Hi-Fi equipment operates has already been said in Section 1.3 [14, 15]. A minimum requirement for amplifiers used for home studio purposes (Hi-Fi) [4] is, for instance, a frequency transmission range from 40 to 16,000 c/s. For linear inputs the maximum permissible transmission error at 1,000 c/s is about 1.5 dB, and for filters about 2 dB. An error of 6 dB was measured under full-drive conditions. As the name already suggests, these are minimum requirements, for these figures certainly do not imply that no transmission takes place above 16,000 c/s. The frequency range of musical instruments, voices and other sound sources, must be taken into account. This is made particularly clear in Fig. 2.23 [7]. Secondary sound effects accompanying the initial blow or strike on instruments are included. One of the universal complaints is [27]: 'Many sound amateurs and music lovers are needlessly left in the dark as regards the characteristics of their, often high-class, reproduction equipment. They cannot make up their mind when purchasing new equipment because they simply do not know what demands to make. This is also the problem facing the designer when developing new installations.'

When reading the further explanations given in this section it must be borne in mind that the question forming the heading of Section 1.3 has been clearly answered in favour of stereophony. Otherwise matters like reproduction quality and corresponding subjects need not be considered. This does not eliminate thc question of what demands must be made when procuring an electro-acoustic or Hi-Fi installation. Especially buyers without any expert knowledge base their choice on non-technical aspects such as

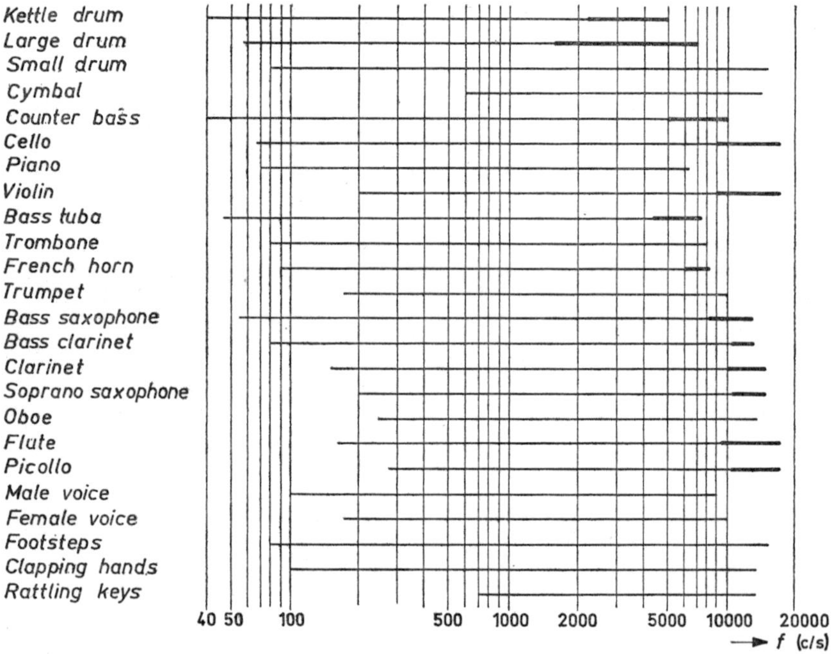

Fig. 2.23. Frequency range of various musical instruments, voices and other sounds. The secondary sounds produced when blowing or striking an instrument are indicated with the thick line

price, dimensions or appearance, etc., only to make changes afterwards involving extra costs. Satisfaction or dissatisfaction is usually felt after the installation has been used for some time.

Table 2.7 gives the minimum power output in absolutely quiet rooms. The values are only valid for rooms in which there is absolute silence. For establishments open to the public these values must be multiplied by a factor 2 — 5 for medium interference levels, and by a factor 5 — 20 for higher interference levels [13].

TABLE 2.7

Room volume (m^3)	highly damped room (W)	normally damped room (W)	resounding room/hall (W)
100 — 500	2 — 4	1 — 3	0.5 — 1.5
500 — 5,000	5 — 30	1 — 15	0.8 — 3
above 5,000	above 40	above 20	above 5

Let us consider, for example, a room 25 m long, 16 m wide and 10 m high. The volume of this room is then 4,000 m^3. If it should be a resounding church hall, the required output would be about 5 W. For a noisy restaurant or taproom of equal volume 35 W would perhaps be just enough. It may serve as a rule that there is no harm in being generous in calculating the output power needed of an amplifier. However, this must not be exaggerated.

A stereo amplifier type AG 9016 is most suitable for normal conditions in a medium-sized living room. It operates with electron tubes and has an output power of 2×2 W. The circuit diagram of this amplifier is given in Fig. 2.24 [28]. This is merely an example, for there is not sufficient space in this book for a whole collection of circuit diagrams. As already mentioned, a stereo amplifier must always be a twin Hi-Fi amplifier, to be dealt with in some detail elsewhere [15]. Another category of amplifiers also deserves special attention, namely those operating without output transformers.

The transformerless output stage has been developed in order to avoid the considerable amount of distortion introduced by the output transformer (see Chapter 6). By thus eliminating a component which has several disadvantages it is possible to design stable output circuits in which the distortion is but a fraction of that caused by the preceding stages. An output pentode (EL 86) was developed for tube circuits. Loudspeakers with

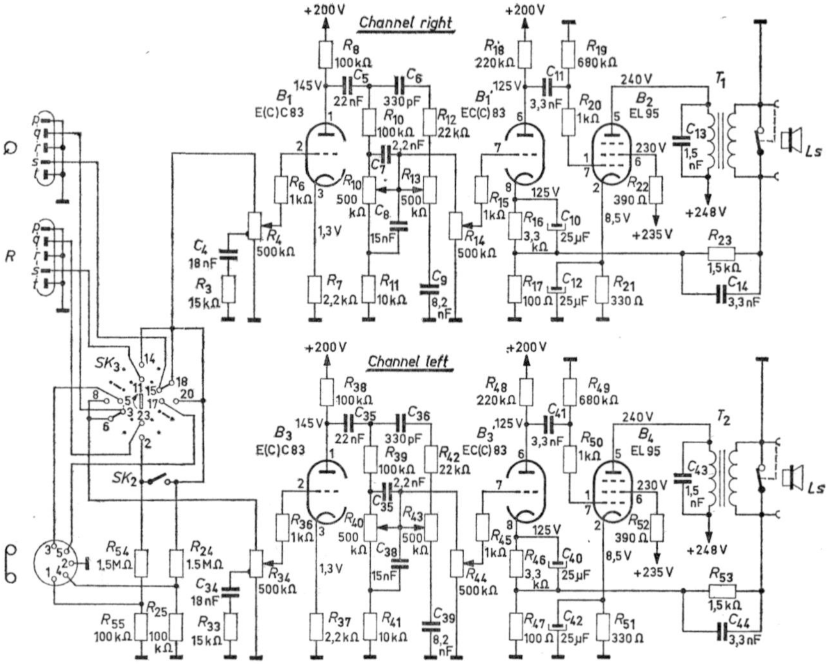

Fig. 2.24. Circuit diagram of a stereo amplifier AC 9016. For the sake of clarity the power supply has been left out. The output power is 2×2 W

an impedance higher than used so far were then required and loudspeaker impedances of 400 Ω and 800 Ω were accordingly produced. Two tubes EL 86 appropriately connected can supply an 800 Ω loudspeaker with a power of 10 W [29]. Further developments in the field of transistors and transistor-driven circuits have in the meantime led to similar transistor stages without output transformer [30, 31]. Fig. 2.25 shows the circuit diagram of one of the (identical) amplifier channels. The output power per amplifier is 10 W.

The last link in the reproduction chain is the loudspeaker. It is not possible for technicians to adjust its mechanism; they must accept it as an invariable unit. This is all the more a reason why a loudspeaker should be carefully selected for its purpose. For loudspeakers used in Hi-Fi installations there are also minimum requirements [4]. Usually the mechanic depends on data supplied by the manufacturer, as it is quite impossible for him to carry out all tests with the measuring equipment normally in his possession.

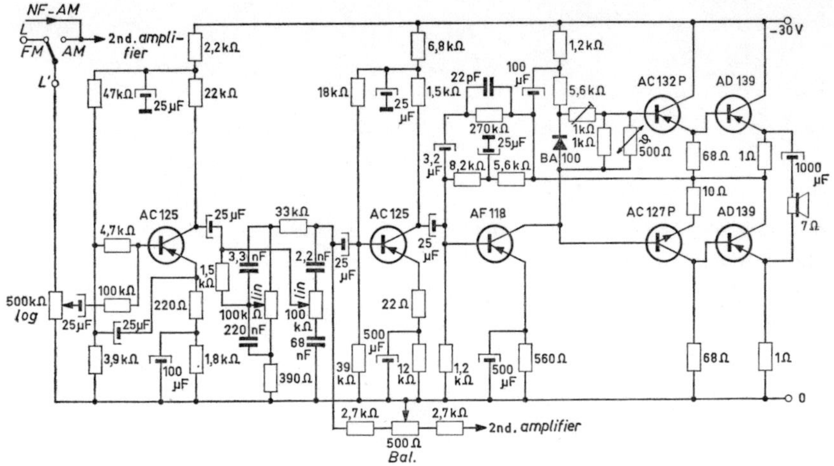

Fig. 2.25. Circuit diagram of a transistorised amplifier channel. The output power per channel is 10 W

But even if it were possible to take these measurements, there might still be surprising differences due to individual subjective approaches, as will become clear from the following example [32]. Two loudspeaker boxes of different volumes were subjected to a sound test. The sound pressure curves, the non-linear distortions, and also the amplitudes of the two loudspeaker boxes were practically identical. Surprisingly, the measuring instrument indicated a better bass sound pressure curve for the smaller of the two boxes. Both loudspeakers had the same impedance and were alternately fed from the same amplifier, they were adjusted to equal sound levels and hidden from the listeners; they were, however, given different numbers. The sound test involved pieces of music containing critical passages. Not only were the boxes differently evaluated, but the listeners all agreed that the number representing the smaller box gave a greater volume of bass notes. When the measuring results were compared, none of the listeners could give an explanation of the difference between the measuring results — which afterwards were proved to be correct — and the sound impression obtained.

Manufacturers seldom give data on distortion for the simple reason that for the dynamic loudspeaker most commonly used, there is no measure either for non-frequency-dependent distortion or for distortion which changes linearly with frequency [33]. The distortion of such loudspeakers, which should at 1,000 c/s, for instance, be less than 1 %, can suddenly become disturbing at frequencies no higher than 1,100 c/s. This phenomenon is due to partial oscillations of the membrane which will make only piston-like movements in the lower frequency range. The frequencies at which these partial oscillations occur are different for each loudspeaker type and size.

This is quite different, however, from distortion caused by an overdriven speech coil, particularly in the vicinity of the resonance frequency of the loudspeaker. In this case the remedy lies in the hands of the person installing the loudspeaker. But, it should be pointed out that the manufacturer of loudspeaker boxes should have already taken the necessary measures.

What influence then can technicians exercise on loudspeakers? The answer is unambiguous: They can only adjust the position of the loudspeakers and this is precisely what is done in stereo reproduction. Fig. 2.26 shows a suitable loudspeaker arrangement for stereophonic reproduction. An impression of direction is given by an intensity and phase difference between the two loudspeaker systems, or rather, by the phase and intensity difference as experienced by the listener stationed between the loudspeakers [1]. If the differences experienced between the two loudspeakers are true reflections of actual differences, the listener must be seated at equal distances from the two loudspeakers, that is to say in the centre of the imaginary line connecting the two loudspeakers. If more people want to join, they should in theory be seated behind each other. At first this would perhaps seem very amusing, but it would certainly not add to sociability. Therefore the use of loudspeakers having certain directional characteristics is recommended so that the listeners can be seated anywhere behind the point where the centre lines of the loudspeakers intersect (see Fig. 2.26).

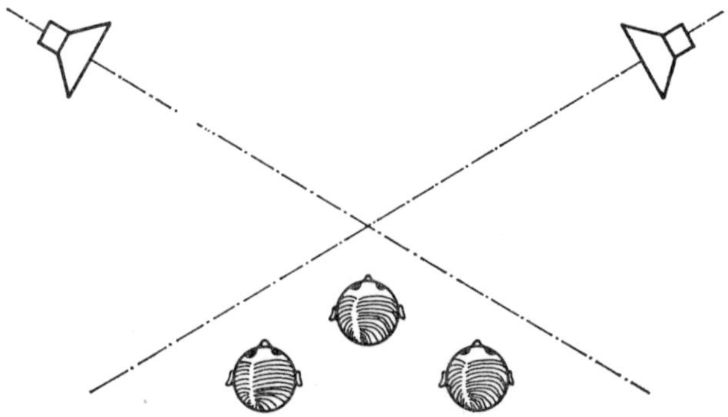

Fig. 2.26. Principle of a suitable loudspeaker arrangement for stereophonic sound reproduction

Fig. 2.27 shows how sound is transmitted in a hall. A listener *H* [11] obtains the strongest directional impression when the sound source seems to move about between the two loudspeakers. For listener *HW* the apparent movement of the sound source between the two loudspeakers is relatively less. This is analogous to the effect referred to in section 1.3 about listeners who are satisfied with a back seat in a concert hall because they fail to hear any difference due to position.

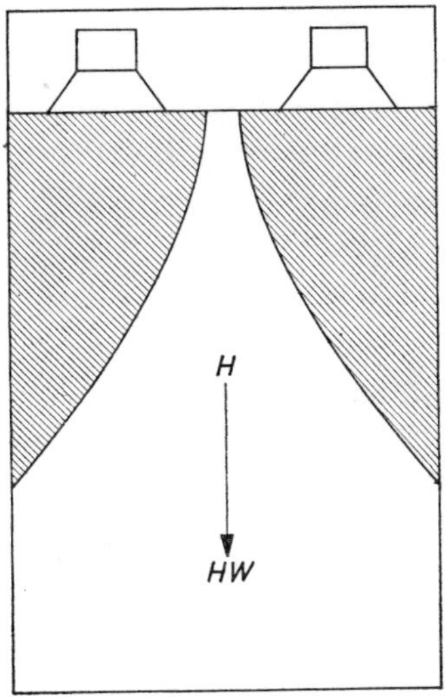

Fig. 2.27. Application of the principle from Fig. 2.26 in a hall

The analytic quality of our hearing does not depend only on amplitude reflection, frequency and the form of the sound waves, but also on the location of the sound source in a hall, that is to say, its distance and direction with respect to the listeners [34]. Accoıding to some publications short distances ranging from 1 m to 2 m are roughly estimated with a maximum accuracy of about 10 cm. If the distance is increased to about 3 m, the judging accuracy improves by almost 100%, while at a distance of 4 m it decreases again, although it remains better than for a distance of 2 m. It should, however, be noted that the ear is a betteı judge of distance for a moving than for a stationary object. This leads to the conclusion that the most favourable distance between listener and loudspeaker is about 3 m.

A limiting factor for Hi-Fi and stereophonic reproduction is, or may be, the fact that housewives will not permit their livingrooms to be defaced by the necessary loudspeaker boxes and leads [27]. This does not imply that the listeners should be banished from the livingroom to enjoy natural sound reproduction in solitude. On the contrary, musical entertainment in company is quite feasible, as in most cases it is possible to choose a loudspeaker model which can be suitably installed without interfering with the aesthetics of the surroundings. This, however, is not always an easy matter with stereophony! Sometimes it may be necessary to mount both loudspeakers in one and the same cabinet, which can be done as shown in Fig. 2.28. A test is made by playing a record of a small jazz band (piano, drums and sax) for an audience of twelve. The audience is requested to indicate what in its opinion are the actual positions of the different instruments on a plan of the room. The lay-out is shown in Fig. 2.28 (P = piano, D = drums, S = saxophone).

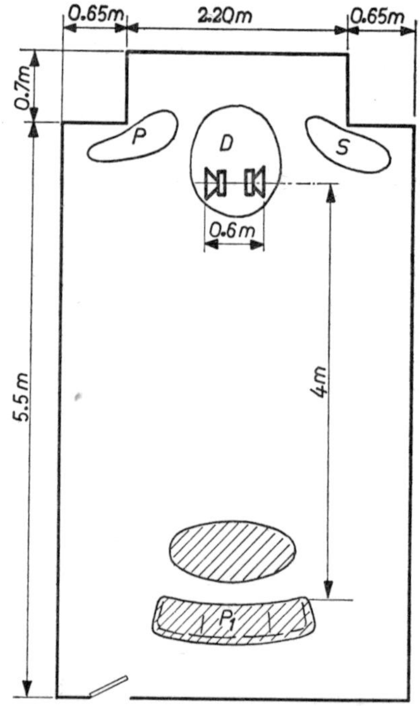

Fig. 2.28. Test arrangement to determine the apparent locations of musical instruments for stereophonic sound reproduction

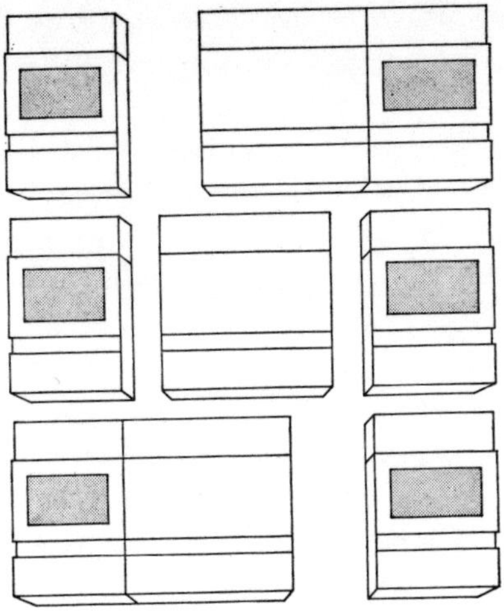

Fig. 2.29. Capella Stereo Cabinet with different arrangement of loudspeaker boxes

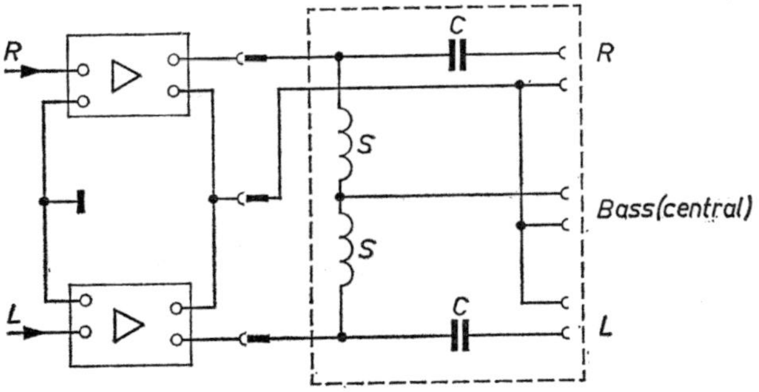

Fig. 2.30. Principle of the stereo filter. It allows the low frequencies to be fed to a central loudspeaker driven by both channels since these frequencies give hardly any lateral impression

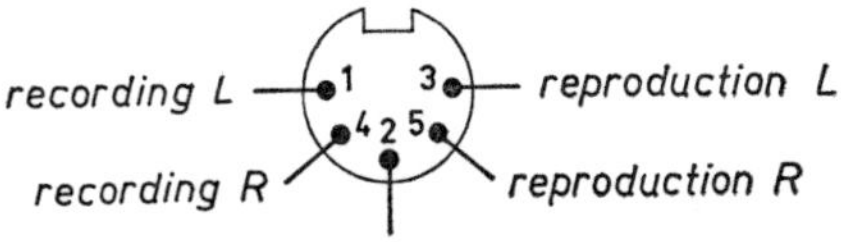

Fig. 2.31. Pin arrangement of a DIN-plug as used for record and tape equipment (recording and reproduction)

The result of this method of testing by no means implies that there are no better loudspeaker arrangements; it should merely be regarded as one solution to a problem.

A good solution both technically and aesthetically is the Capella Stereo Cabinet (F 8 D41 A). The drawings of Fig. 2.29 are but simple illustrations of the various arrangements that can be made by means of a cabinet with two separate loudspeaker boxes [5]. The cabinet contains the radio set and a record player. At the top there is also room to accommodate a stereo tape recorder.

Since owing to intensity differences low frequencies give little impression of lateral spread, they can, in stereophonic reproduction, be reproduced via a central loudspeaker. An example is given in Fig. 2.30. Frequency distribution takes place by means of a filter which, because it is often used in stereo equipment, is sometimes called a stereo filter.

The record player and tape recorder are connected to the stereo amplifier, see Fig. 2.31, with plugs (DIN 41524), see Fig. 2.3a. Plug pins not used remain free; pins 1 and 4, for instance, when using a UKW tuner. Other plugs have been designed for the connection of loudspeakers (DIN 41529). They have a flat central pin and a cylindrical side pin. This ensures that the correct terminals of the loudspeaker are connected to the amplifier.

CHAPTER 3

HF STEREOPHONY

Section 1.1 is introduced with the citation: 'Man is naturally equipped for stereophony' [5]. The same citation is also quite applicable to this chapter dealing with HF stereophony. If stereophony is regarded as the obvious and natural step following the development of HiFi technique [20], and the LF field supplies adequate proof of this, the same applies, of course, to the HF field. It would indeed be absurd had technical progress stopped at this point. On the other hand, HF or radio stereophony had to be almost perfect from the moment it was introduced, because it would always be possible to compare it with good monophonic radio transmissions and gramophone recordings of excellent quality.

3.1 Development

It took quite some time to develop HF stereophony into what it is to-day. The first stereophonic radio programmes were broadcast via the usual medium of the two R.F. channels. The advantage was that those programmes could also be received with ordinary monophonic receivers, but this was only an apparent advantage. A drawback was that two, if possible absolutely equal, receivers were needed as one receiver was not sufficient for stereophonic reception. One receiver reproduced but one sound channel, and is thus not enough for either monophonic or monaural programmes. It would only be 'half' stereophony.

There were further disadvantages. There would not have been enough room for two stereo transmitters in the already overcrowded medium wave band. Moreover, the narrow bandwidths of the medium wave transmitters were not suitable for Hi-Fi quality. The only answer for HF stereophony was the USW band.

This does not mean that all endeavours to achieve HF stereophony have been in vain. Especially in the Netherlands use has been made of the two-transmitter system for stereophonic broadcasts. A uniform method (Section 3.2) was introduced later. A stereophonic radio play was broadcast for the first time on January 26th, 1960. This play was a thriller 'Even schuilen' ('Let's wait a while') by Eileen Burke and Lione Stewart adapted by Léon Povel.

The pilot tone system, which will be discussed later (see Section 3.2), allows stereo programmes of Hi-Fi quality to be broadcast by one USW FM transmitter. These programmes are also suitable for monophonic reception; they are compatible (see Section 2.2). This method was introduced in the Netherlands in May 1963. After a few preliminary experiments Germany began using this system in 1963; first in Berlin and later in Hamburg to be followed by other places in West Germany [35, 36].

There was already an extensive network of USW stations [37].

It is thus seen [38] that at the beginning of 1965 a total of 25 transmitters of 5 radio stations were broadcasting stereophonic programmes in the range of seven West Germany radio stations. By mid 1965 another 20 transmitters had followed so that in the area covered by the seven stations mentioned above, 80—100% of the radio listeners could enjoy stereophonic programmes. This means first and foremost that at the transmitting end certain technical conditions had to be fulfilled. There are still quite a few differences between the stereophonic programmes of various stations. They range from purely experimental broadcasts to entertainment music, radio plays, orchestral concerts and operas. There are also differences between the parts of the total radio time reserved for stereophonic programmes.

The Netherlands too, are intensely active in the field of radio stereophony. Channels 19 and 33 (power of 50 kW) of the stations Lopik I and II respectively, have been used for stereo broadcasts since the beginning of 1964. Stereo broadcasts form an integral part of the radio programme. The studios are fully equipped. The world-famous Amsterdam Concertgebouw is equipped with a stereo control desk so that stereo broadcasts can always take place from there [35].

The pilot tone system described in the following chapter is now universally used. In April 1966 this system was accepted by the American FCC (Federal Communications Commission) as the standard for the technical modulation requirements for FM transmitters used for stereophonic broadcasts [39]. Long and exhaustive investigations into many proposed HF stereo systems were carried out before this decision was made. From the original 16 proposals 8 systems, which could logically be classified into 6 groups, were selected. In the course of 1966 the results of extensive investigations and trial tape recordings made according to six different methods were submitted to the FCC. The FCC then decided on a method based on the almost identical principles of the General Electric Company and the Zenith Radio Corporation systems. Therefore the pilot tone system is sometimes also called the FCC system. The EBU (European Broadcasting Union) also accepted this method for Europe.

3.2 Pilot tone system

As already stated above, only one transmitter is used to broadcast the two HF stereo channels. Obviously, the two signals cannot simply be added. Even with stereo records, which like other records have but one sound groove, both walls of that groove are used. Let us see, however, what would happen if the communicating link between transmitter and receiver were alternately used for the *R* signal (right signal) and the *L* signal (left signal). If the change-over frequency is sufficiently high, the human ear will no longer perceive the change-over.

This and other considerations led to the pilot tone system. The principle is illustrated in Fig. 3.1 [40]. There is a switch at the transmitting end and another at the receiving end. These switches change over between the left and right channel at an operating frequency of 38 kc/s. This action is somewhat like that of the well-known vibrator converter, but unlike the vibrator or chopper there is no mechanical coupling between the two switches to ensure synchronism.

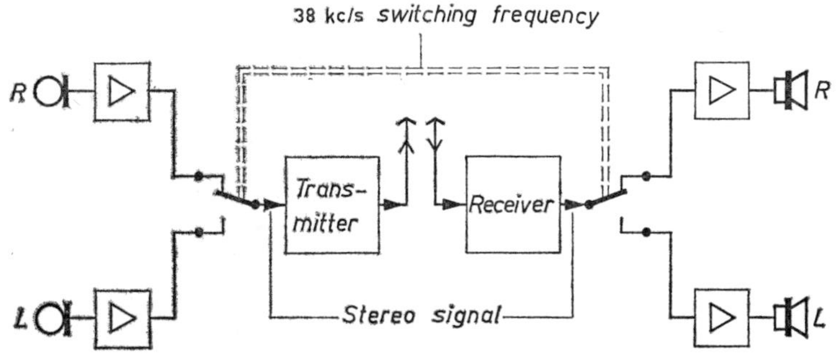

Fig. 3.1. Principle of the pilot tone system

But in this system too, there must of course be synchronism. This is achieved with a special tone transmitted with the normal signal. This tone, termed the pilot tone, is imperceptible to the human ear. Hence the name 'pilot tone system'.

Fig. 3.2 shows the principle of this system which is also called Time Multiplex System because the channels are switched over at regular time intervals. The stereo signal must be completed by the pilot tone; it is therefore referred to as the complete stereo signal. This implies that the switches in Fig. 3.1 need not be mechanically coupled, since electronic switches which can be synchronised are used instead. This is explained in Fig. 3.2.

Assuming for a moment that no stereo signal is transmitted, and taking the 19 kc/s pilot tone generator on the transmitter end as the starting point, the circuit operates as follows. The signal from this generator is added to the stereo signal, and at the same time, after its frequency has been doubled to 38 kc/s, it also serves to operate the electronic switches. Similarly, at the receiving end the 19 kc/s pilot tone is filtered out from the sound signal, but is also doubled so that it serves to operate an electronic switch.

So far everything seems very simple. The switching system for HF stereophony, however, is not quite so simple. It is therefore necessary to give a more detailed explanation of the pilot tone system.

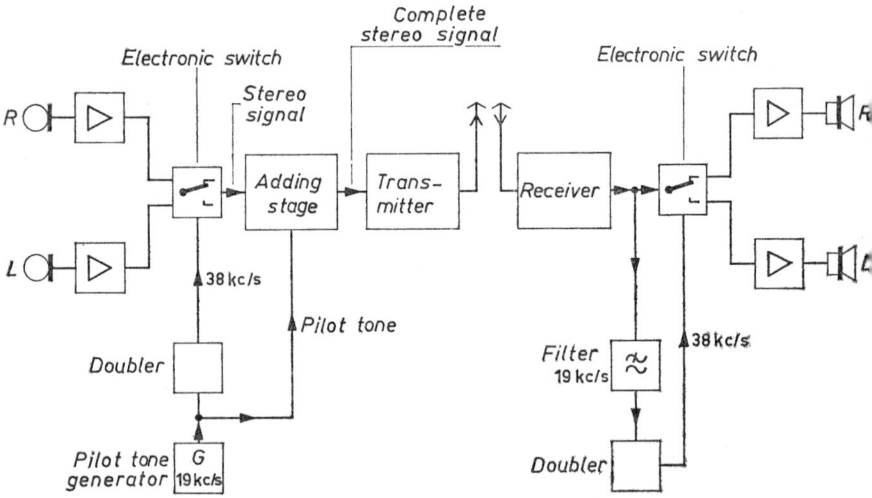

Fig. 3.2. More detailed principle of the pilot tone system

3.2.1 *Principle*

The European pilot tone system used for stereophonic radio shows a great resemblance to the standardised American FCC system. The system embodies the following features which are illustrated in Figs 3.3a-f [39].

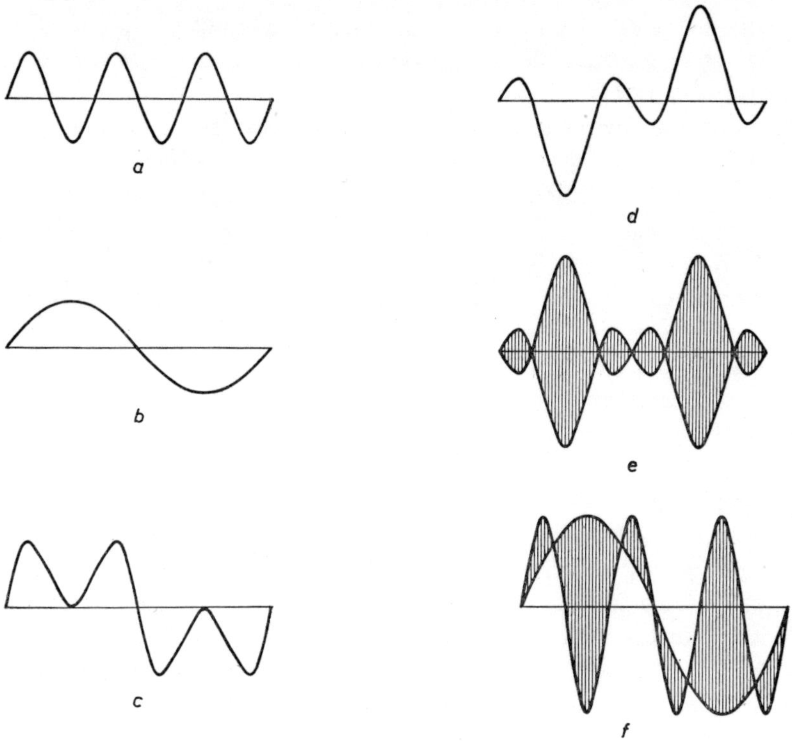

Fig. 3.3. Signal forms in pilot tone system

- The sum of *L* and *R* information of the NF stereo signal forms the modulating signal of the main channel (see Section 3.2.2).
- The carrier is modulated 8—10% by a pilot tone of 19 kc/s ± 2 c/s.
- The second harmonic of the pilot tone forms a sub-carrier passing the time axis simultaneously with the pilot signal in the positive sense.
- The sub-carrier is amplitude-modulated; it is suppressed to less than 1% by the modulation range of the main carrier. This suppression does not, however, include the side bands.

— The difference between the *L* and *R* information of the NF stereo signal represents the modulating signal for the sub-carrier with a bandwidth from 30 c/s — 15 kc/s, and a pre-emphasis of 75 μs. For monophonic operation the modulating signal of the main channel (sum of *L* and *R* information), has the same bandwidth and pre-emphasis.

— The two AM sidebands of the sub-carrier offer a frequency band of maximum 45% for the main carrier when only one of the two signals (*L* or *R*) is available. Consequently, sum and difference signals can modulate the main carrier up to 90%.

— The amplitude characteristics of the sub-carrier and the main carrier, including pre-emphasis, should not differ by more than 0.3 dB. The maximum permissible deviation between the phase curves is about 3°. If these requirements are met, a minimum cross-talk suppression of 29.7 dB can be obtained throughout the range from 50 c/s to 15 kc/s.

— As regards distortion, the sub-carrier must satisfy the same requirements as the main carrier; also for monophonic operation. For the complete system these values are:

50 — 100 c/s:	3.5%
100 c/s — 7.5 kc/s:	2.5%
7.5 — 15 kc/s:	3.%

— According to FCC standards so-called background music or SCA programmes (Subsidiary Communications Authorisation) may be transmitted via a second sub-channel. This refers to an additional entertainment programme fully independent of the stereo programme, put at the disposal of paying subscribers like department stores etc. This is a facility which is not used in Europe. Here the vacant modulation range is also used for stereophonic programmes. The sub-carrier used for the extra channel, also called SCA channel, should not modulate the main carrier by more than 10%. At a 100% modulation of the main carrier, crosstalk suppression between the SCA channel and each of the stereo channels should be better than 60 dB.

3.2.2 The stereo signal

Now that the principle has been sufficiently explained, the stereo signal needs further investigation. In general the microphones for the *L* and *R* signals receive sounds of different intensities or amplitudes (see Section 4.1). Let us assume that for the moment there is but one single sound source which is not located at the acoustic centre between the two microphones and that

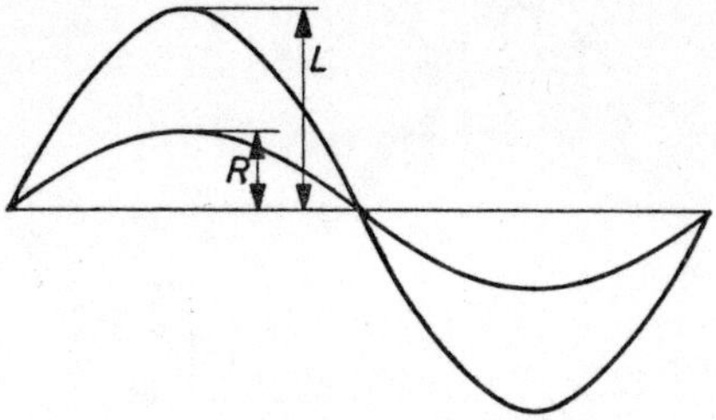

Fig. 3.4. Two voltages of equal phase but different amplitudes

it radiates a note of 4.22 kc/s. As illustrated by Fig. 3.4 the result is two voltages of equal phase but of different amplitudes since the microphone is not located at the acoustic centre between the microphones. In this example it is assumed that the *L* amplitude is the greater. If the *L* and *R* information constantly switch over at a switching frequency of 38 kc/s, the result is a graph as shown in Fig. 3.5. Notwithstanding the interlacing of the two signals the information contained is quite intelligible. In one complete cycle of the 4.22 kc/s note nine switching operations have taken place ($4.22 \times 9 = 38$).

This stereo signal consists of two signals of equal frequencies but different amplitudes which are made to alternate at a frequency of 38 kc/s. The stereo transmitter must, of course, also transmit other frequencies. The spectrum is even actually expanded by the 38 kc/s switching process. In the following sections it will be explained what frequencies the stereo signal contains.

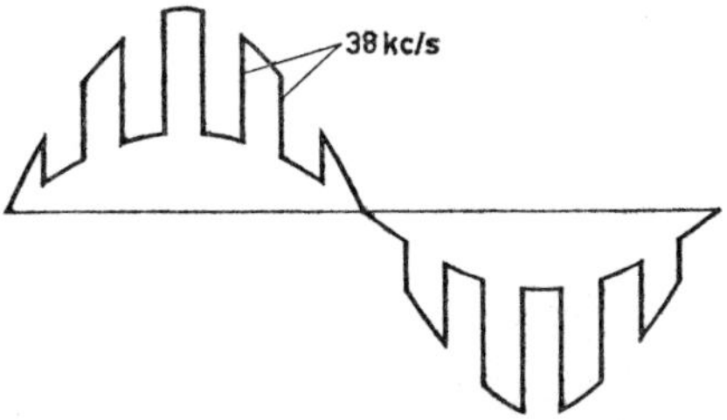

Fig. 3.5. *L* and *R* signals alternating at a frequency of 38 kc/s

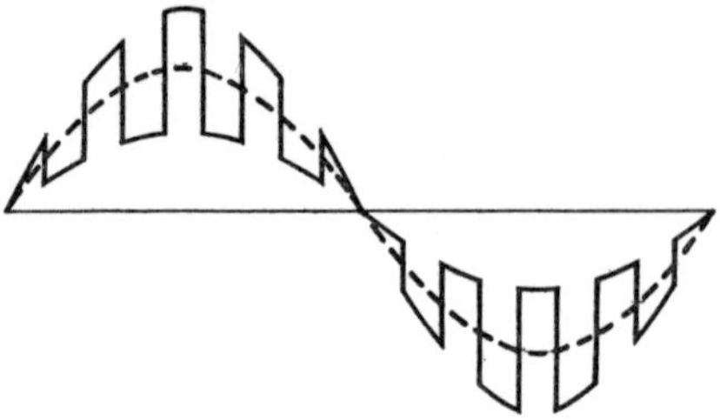

Fig. 3.6. 38 kc/s square-wave signal of Fig. 3.5 with corresponding sine wave (broken line)

3.2.3 Sum and difference signal

If fractions of the *L* and *R* signals are alternately transmitted, the frequencies of these signals are no longer alone. We shall now see what else can be found in the stereo signal.

Fig. 3.5 illustrated how the transmitted stereo signal is formed by alternating the *L* and *R* signal at a change-over frequency of 38 kc/s. This continuous alternation causes a square wave signal having a frequency of 38 kc/s, oscillating round a sine wave as shown in Fig. 3.6 (broken line). The character of the stereo signal now becomes clear. The system can also be regarded as two series-connected generators G_1 and G_2 as depicted in Fig. 3.7. Generator G_1 supplies the 38 kc/s voltage of a special form (see Section 3.3.1). Generator G_2 supplies an alternating voltage corresponding to the broken sine wave in Fig. 3.6. Addition of these two signals gives the stereo signal of Fig. 3.6. This imaginary experiment, which could easily be checked with two oscilloscopes, supplies sufficient proof that addition of the two generator signals gives a stereo signal. On the one hand this means that a stereo signal can be obtained by adding the instantaneous values of the generator signals. On the other hand, however, it also means that the stereo signal contains both the generator signals. They can be found by an appropriate analysis of the stereo signal.

The broken curve in Figs 3.6 and 3.7 can easily be regarded as a voltage containing a 38 kc/s square-wave 'hum' component. Now imagine that such a voltage is applied to an amplifier which includes several filters. If the output of such an amplifier is investigated with an oscilloscope the useful signal seems to be enveloped by the hum voltage, the useful signal corresponding to the 38 kc/s signal from generator G_1, while the hum can be regarded as the alternating voltage from generator G_2.

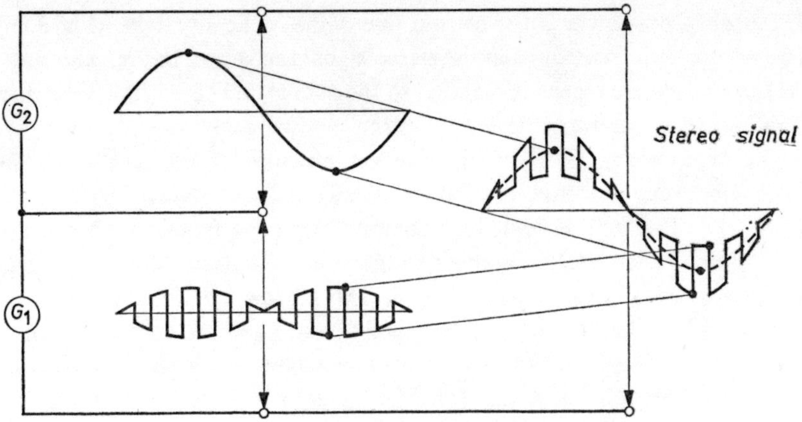

Fig. 3.7. Symbolic diagram of how the stereo signal is formed

Fig. 3.8 does indeed show the stereo signal with its two components, but still without the superimposed pilot tone. The outer envelope caused by the continuous changing-over of the 38 kc/s square-wave voltage forms the *L* signal. The inner envelope consists of the *R* signal of smaller amplitude.

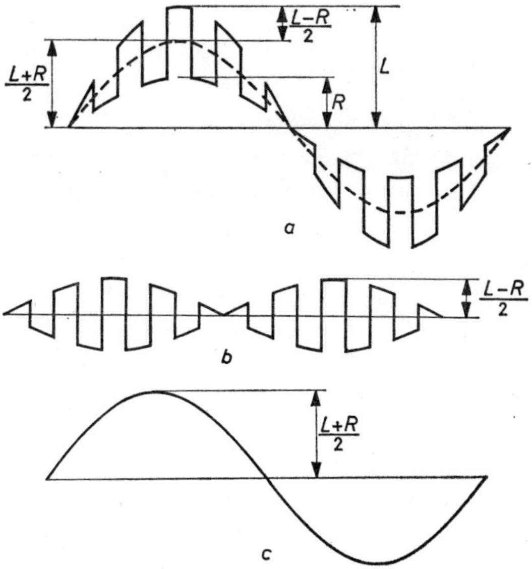

Fig. 3.8. Stereo signal (a), difference signal (b) and sum signal (c)

The broken-line curve is the neutral line of the 38 kc/s voltage. (Fig. 3.8a). The two voltages contained in the stereo signal are shown in Fig. 3.8b and c [41]. Monophonic receivers respond to the sum signal ($L + R$) of Fig. 3.8c. This signal is therefore referred to as the mono signal.

The difference signal ($L - R$) is also a measure of the amplitude difference between L and R. For an acoustically balanced signal, the amplitude ($L = R$) in Fig. 3.8b is zero. In that case there is no transient when L and R are interchanged. The 38 kc/s voltage will only occur when there is an amplitude difference between L and R. The greater the deviation from the acoustic centre the greater will be this difference and the greater the maximum amplitude of the 38 kc/s voltage. The maximum amplitude is, in fact, $(L - R)/2$. The term 2 in this formula merely serves to find the absolute numerical value. Usually the terms difference signal or ($L - R$) signal are used.

Summarising it can be said that except for the acoustic central signal ($L = R$), the stereo signal includes the difference signal ($L - R$) containing the directional information. On the other hand there is always the sum signal ($L + R$), no matter from what direction the sound is received. This represents the monophonic information as received by the mono radio sets, and as previously mentioned it is therefore sometimes also referred to as the mono signal.

3.2.4 Frequency spectrum of the stereo signal

Fig. 3.9 shows the frequency spectrum of the stereo signal without any reference as yet being made to the amplitudes of individual frequencies. The main channel transmits the sum of the L and R information of the LF stereo signal. It covers the same range as used for FM radio. Consequently it is possible to receive stereo programmes with monophonic receivers. Any further information contained in the spectrum is only applicable to stereo reception. A 38 kc/s sub-carrier is amplitude modulated by the difference between the L and R information of the LF stereo signal. Complete transmission of the sub-carrier is not essential to ensure that the most efficient use is made of the modulation range of the transmitter. Since owing to closely neighbouring signal frequencies a strongly suppressed sub-carrier can only be reproduced at considerable expense, this sub-carrier is suppressed almost entirely. Instead, a 19 kc/s pilot tone is transmitted to demodulate the sub-carrier in the receiver. The pilot tone lies beyond the signal range.

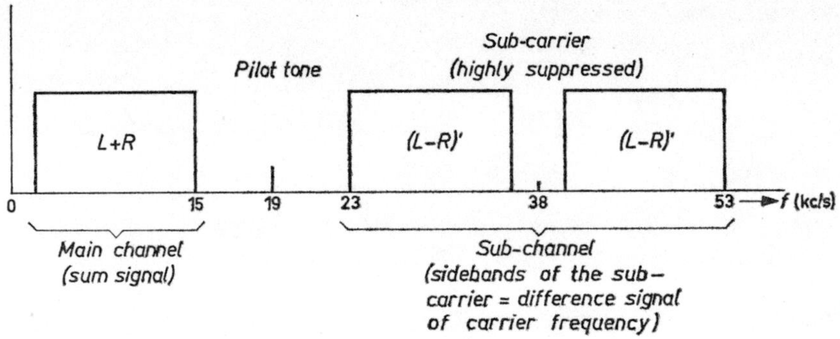

Fig. 3.9. Frequency spectrum of the stereo signal

Fig. 3.10 [42] shows the relationship between the phases of the sub-carrier and the pilot tone. The two tones are so phased that each second zero crossing of the sub-carrier coincides with a zero crossing of the pilot tone. This happens in such a way that at each simultaneous zero crossing the sub-carrier crosses the time axis in the positive direction. This phasing is necessary to avoid any ambiguity regarding the character of the transmitted L and R information.

In contrast to Fig. 3.9, Fig. 3.11 also shows the transmitter modulation. The pilot tone modulates the transmitter by 10%. The remaining 90% of the total depth is available for the transmission of the main carrier and the sub-carrier. These can be fully modulated by the maximum sum signal (see Sec-

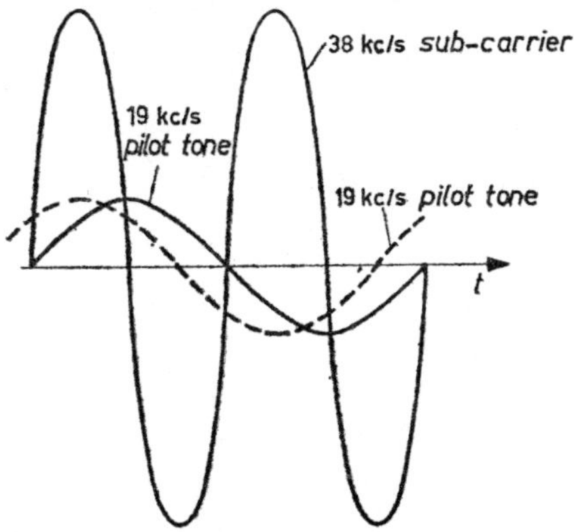

Fig. 3.10. Relationship between the phases of the sub-carrier and the pilot tone

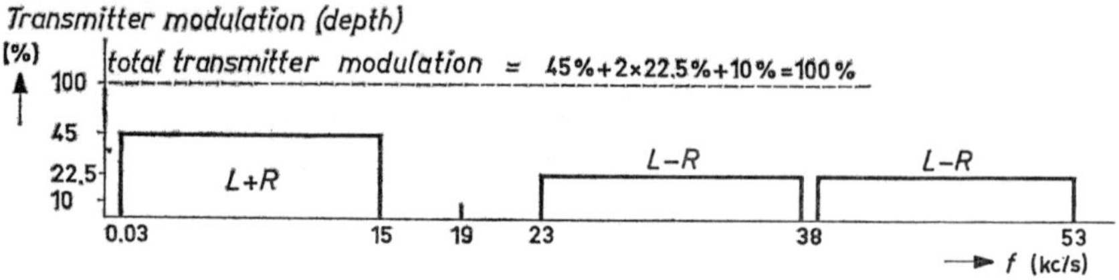

Fig. 3.11. Frequency spectrum of the stereo signal including transmitter modulation

tion 3.2.3), since the difference signal requires no more extra depth than that by which the range of the sum signal is shortened. The remaining 90% of the modulation depth is equally divided between the maximum L and R information. If the sum signal from a stereo transmitter is received on a mono radio set, the signal-to-noise ratio is but 1 dB less than for usual mono transmission. The mutual augmentation of the available modulation range between the sum and difference signals is explained in Fig. 3.12. If the L signal is kept at its maximum level u_{max}, and the R signal varies between the values $-u_{max}$ and $+u_{max}$, the level of the sum signal will vary between 0 and $2u_{max}$, while the difference signal varies between $2u_{max}$ and 0. Together they always form the maximum level of $2u_{max}$. This corresponds with a transmitter modulation of 90%. Fig. 3.12 illustrates the following special cases:

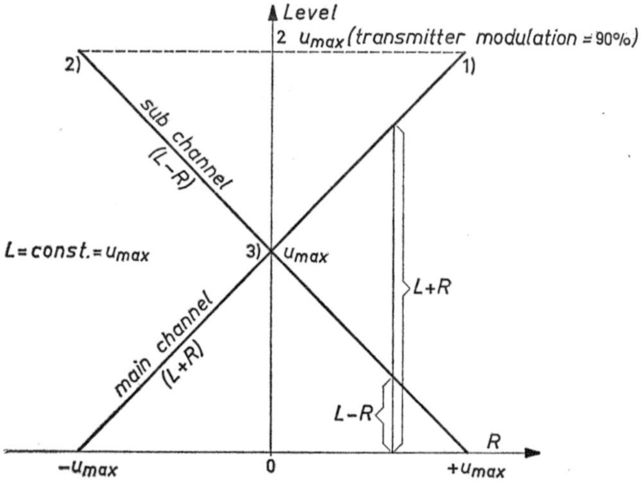

Fig. 3.12. Mutual augmentation of the available modulation depth between sum and difference signal

1. $R = L = u_{max}$; the transmitter is modulated to 90% via the main carrier and 0% via the sub-carrier.
2 $R = -L = -u_{max}$; the transmitter is modulated to 90% via the sub-carrier and 0% by the main carrier.
3. $R = 0$, $L = u_{max}$; the transmitter is modulated to 45% via the main carrier and 45% via the sub-carrier.

The considerations of this section apply not only to amplitudes of sinusoidal L and R signals of equal frequency and phase, but in general to the instantaneous values of random L and R signals. This also implies that the 90% modulation depth cannot be exceeded as long as the instantaneous value of L plus R information does not exceed $|u_{max}|$.

3.2.5 Compatibility

As the expression 'compatible' used in the foregoing is often but quite wrongly interpreted as 'acceptable', a few lines may be devoted with advantage to explaining the true meaning of the word. In the case of stereophonic radio the word 'compatible' always implies that stereo programmes can also be received on an ordinary monophonic radio set. Owing to its design, such a radio set can of course only reproduce monophonically, but this is exactly what is meant. From what has already been said about the stereo signal the reader will now be quite clear concerning the compatibility of the pilot tone method.

In view of the fact that an ordinary radio receiver can reproduce signals of frequencies up to a maximum of about 15 kc/s, higher frequencies being severely suppressed due to de-emphasis, for example, it will become clear from Figs 3.9 and 3.11 that practically only the sum signal or mono signal is reproduced. Of the total frequency spectrum of the complete stereo signal only the sum signal is transmitted, while the pilot tone and the difference signal are lost. Consequently the pilot system is compatible; the L and R information are both reproduced by the mono receiver.

Compatability is an essential requirement if only for the reason that there will always be many listeners who are not interested in stereophony (see Section 1.3). Furthermore, in many cases it will not be worth while adapting old types of mono receivers for stereo reception since the costs involved may not always be justified by the results. It should be borne in mind that only in April 1961 the FCC accepted the pilot tone system as the standard (see Section 3.2). That is why it was not until 1961 that set manufacturers could prepare themselves to work to the standard which could also be expected to be adopted in Europe. For the same reason it was not until 1962/63 that definite provisions could be built into radio sets to adapt them for stereo reception, all the more so since at that time it was not clear whether the American system, be it under different conditions, could be used without restriction in Europe.

It is certain, therefore, that for some time to come there will still be mono receivers on the market which cannot be modified for stereo. These may include sets giving excellent LF stereo reproduction but which are not suitable for HF stereophony. On the other hand it will be a considerable time before all radio broadcasts will be stereophonic. It will be clear, therefore, that the question of compatibility was a decisive factor when the pilot tone system was introduced.

3.3 Explanatory notes

To gain a better understanding of the pilot tone system as described in Section 3.2, it may be useful to give a few explanations concerning amplitude modulation (Section 3.3.1), modulating circuits (Section 3.3.2) and amplitude modulation with suppressed carrier (Section 3.3.3). Although these objects can be omitted during a first reading, readers should eventually familiarise themselves with these subjects.

3.3.1 Amplitude modulation

As already explained in Section 3.2.3 the stereo signal — apart from the pilot tone — contains the sum signal which in turn carries pure LF information, and the difference signal with the 38 kc/s voltage and maximum amplitude of $(L - R)/2$ supplying directional information. This difference signal voltage will be closer investigated here. From Fig. 3.13 the following points emerge:

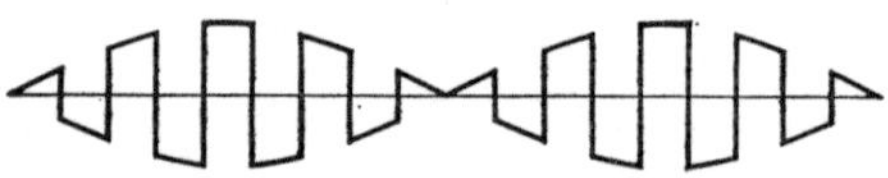

Fig. 3.13. Difference signal

1. The curve is not sinusoidal.
2. The amplitude is not stable.
3. At the point of minimum amplitude the curve does not cross the zero line, but the phase is reversed, i.e. a phase shift of 180° takes place.

Further examination of Fig. 3.13 reveals a certain resemblance to an amplitude modulated oscillation. It is, in fact, a particular case of amplitude modulation, namely amplitude modulation with suppressed carrier. For the sake of clarity we shall discuss the most important details of amplitude modulation.

We speak of amplitude modulation (called AM for short), when the amplitude of a high frequency voltage is modulated by a low frequency oscillation in such a way that both frequency and intensity are affected. In this way, for example, it is possible to broadcast low frequency information on a high frequency carrier, via a transmitter. If such a signal is received and demodulated, the low-frequency information is recovered. As a simple example we will consider the 50 c/s mains voltage as functioning as the carrier (FH), and amplitude-modulated by a voltage having a frequency of 1.5 c/s (LF). First, however, the following features will be explained by means of Fig. 3.14, representing a sinusoidally-modulated carrier oscillation.

1. A modulated carrier oscillation (AM) is a high-frequency voltage whose peak value varies rhythmically according to an LF oscillation.
2. The amplitude of a modulated carrier oscillation varies constantly. The r.m.s. value of the amplitude in the positive as well as in the negative direction is carrier amplitude u_c, represented in Fig. 3.14 by the broken straight line. This constant carrier amplitude is the quiescent amplitude of the transmitter which is increased or reduced by the LF modulation. The carrier amplitude u_c in the diagram can always be found since it is represented by the imaginary zero line of the LF modulation.

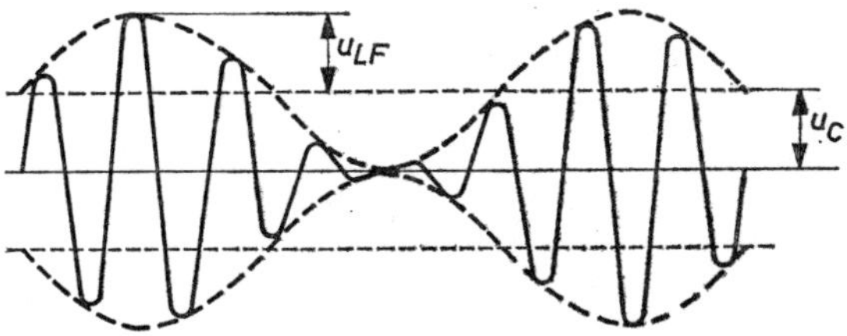

Fig. 3.14. A 50 c/s carrier amplitude modulated by a signal of 1.5 c/s

It is also clear that the carrier amplitude u_c varies with any d.c. component the modulation may contain.

3. The envelope of the carrier oscillation, shown as a broken line, is the LF signal modulated on to the HF carrier. The LF amplitude is always measured from u_c of the carrier amplitude because this corresponds to the zero line of the LF modulation signal.
4. At a modulation depth of 100% the carrier amplitude is reduced to zero.
5. The ratio between LF amplitude u_{LF} and carrier amplitude u_c is called the modulation factor m, and is expressed by

$$m = \frac{u_{LF}}{u_c}$$

In the diagram of Fig. 3.14 the two amplitudes (u_{LF} and u_c) are equal. Consequently $m = 1$; expressed in percentage: $m = 100\%$.

Oscillations which are not purely sinusoidal contain certain harmonics. It will be obvious, therefore, that a high frequency oscillation, no longer sinusoidal due to modulation effects, consists of several sinusoidal oscillations of different frequencies, in addition to the original frequency of the carrier. The presence of components of different frequencies within the spectrum of the amplitude-modulated oscillation can be indicated by means of a simple experiment described below.

The 50 c/s mains frequency can easily be amplitude-modulated. This can be done by periodically switching the mains an and off. A suitable circuit is given in Fig. 3.15. A vibration-type frequency meter with a range from 45 — 55 c/s in steps of 0.5 c/s is connected to a 50 c/s source via a relay contact. The relay magnet is energised by a pulse generator, for instance the trafficator relay of a motorcar, at a frequency of 1.5 c/s. In this case the

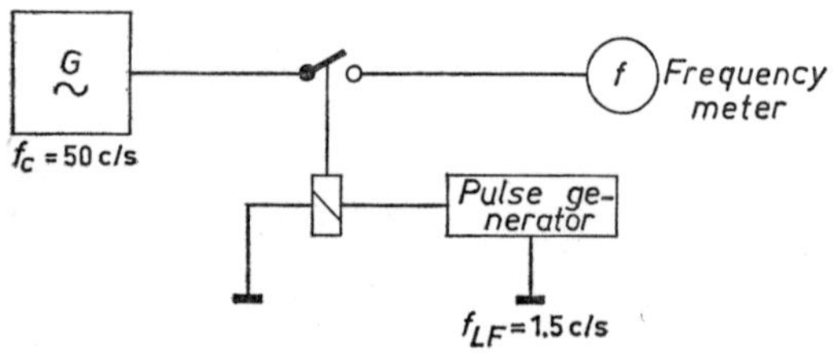

Fig. 3.15. Circuit for amplitude modulation of a 50 c/s carrier by a signal of 1.5 c/s

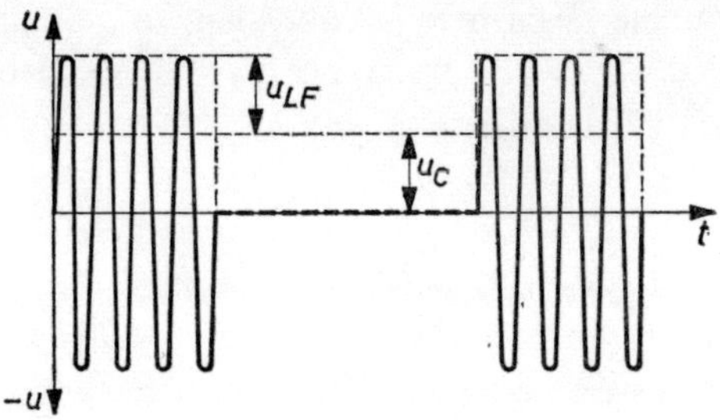

Fig. 3.16. Graph of the voltage applied to the vibrating frequency meter of Fig. 3.15

carrier frequency $f_c = 50$ c/s (mains frequency), and the modulation frequency $f_{LF} = 1.5$ c/s (pulse frequency). The modulated signal now applied to the frequency meter is shown in Fig. 3.16. Fig. 3.17 shows which reeds of the meter are made to vibrate.

One might be inclined to assume that only the 50 c/s reed would vibrate for why should a frequency meter connected to 50 c/s indicate anything but this frequency? However, Fig. 3.17 tells a different story. Certainly the 50 c/s reed vibrates, but the amplitude is not so great as in case of a permanent connection to the 50 c/s source. The reason is that the 50 c/s voltage is not constantly applied, so that the 50 c/s reed adjusts itself to the mean amplitude of the 50 c/s voltage; this is carrier amplitude u_c. This is, however, only one component of the carrier oscillation. It is seen that the 48.5 c/s and 51.5 c/s reeds of the frequency meter are also in vibration. We know that each reed is tuned to a specific frequency as marked on the scale. This frequency is the resonance frequency of the reed, and because of this the reeds can help analyse the carrier oscillation into its components. The two side frequencies of 48.5 and 51.5 c/s caused by modulation are respectively $f_c + f_{LF}$ and

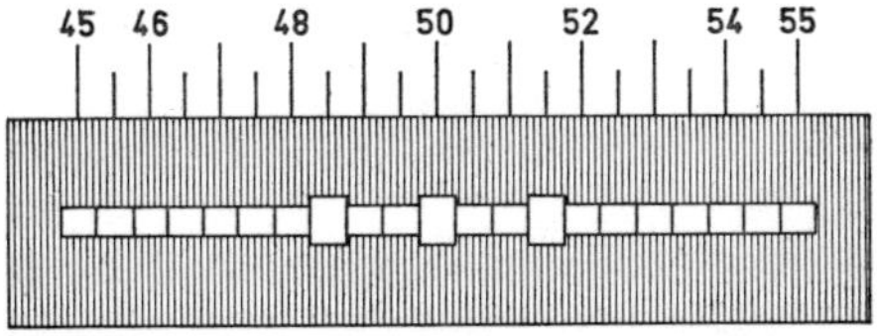

Fig. 3.17. Front view of the reed frequency meter used in Fig. 3.15

$f_c - f_{LF}$. The example given here is equivalent to modulation by a square wave signal with a frequency $f_{LF} = 1.5$ c/s. Therefore the adjacent reeds vibrate at the side frequencies, namely:

$$f_c + f_{LF} = 50 + 1.5 = 51.5 \text{ c/s}$$
$$f_c - f_{LF} = 50 - 1.5 = 48.5 \text{ c/s}$$

During the switching-on period of the 50 c/s voltage the 48.5 and 51.5 c/s reeds are shock-excited and begin to vibrate over half their maximum range. In other words they analyse the modulated oscillation and split it up into two components. Moreover, the deflection of the reeds tells us something about the amplitudes of the side frequencies contained in the modulated 50 c/s oscillation. At full 100% modulation with a purely sinusoidal signal the reed corresponding to the carrier frequency will vibrate over half its maximum range.

Instead of using the switching mechanism etc. described above we could, of course, also obtain amplitude modulation by adding together separately generated carrier and side frequencies. For practical purposes, however, this method is too complicated.

Summarising it can be said that an oscillation modulated 100% by a sinusoidal signal contains three components of the following amplitudes and frequencies.

1. Carrier with an amplitude u_c and a frequency f_c.
2. One side component with an amplitude $u_s = u_c/2$ and a frequency $f_s = f_c + f_{LF}$
3. One side component with an amplitude $u_s = u_c/2$ and a frequency $f_s' = f_c - f_{LF}$.

By suitable means, such as resonant circuits, the amplitude modulated oscillations can be resolved into the three components of which they consist.

Careful observation of the reed frequency meter reveals that the reeds corresponding to 45.5 c/s and 54.5 c/s also give a weak deflection. The reason is that modulation takes place with a square wave voltage instead of a sinusoidal one. Now, in addition to their basic frequency, square wave oscillations contain an indefinite number of harmonics. The third harmonic has a frequency $f = 3f_{LF} = 3 \times 1.5 = 4.5$ c/s. There are also a fifth harmonic (7.5 c/s), a seventh harmonic (10.5 c/s) etc. So if a 50 c/s oscillation is modulated with a square wave signal of 1.5 c/s, all these other frequencies partake in this modulation. As a result there are other side frequencies which can also be calculated. They will also be shown on the frequency meter if they fall within the range of the instrument.

If therefore modulation takes place with non-sinusoidal frequencies, or with a complex of frequencies, these modulation frequencies will contain a whole series of side frequencies thus forming the side bands. For modulation with a pure alternating voltage, that is to say without a d.c. component, the carrier amplitude will be stable. The LF information is then contained in the side bands only.

3.3.2 Modulation circuits

There are several circuits that can be used for amplitude modulation. They are all based on one or other two main principles, viz. the system of multiplicative modulation or the system of additive modulation (mixing).

Amplitude modulation according to the multiplicative principle is obtained by varying the HF amplitude. This can be done, for instance, by periodical switching (see Figs 3.15 and 3.16), by means of a microphone, or by controlling two grids of an electron valve, e.g. a heptode. This system is referred to as multiplicative mixing. Fig. 3.18 illustrates multiplicative modulation by means of a microphone; Fig. 3.19 shows how the same thing is done by controlling two grids of a heptode.

Dealing first with multiplicative modulation, it should be stated that at half the LF amplitude the modulation amplitude is also halved. In other words, the modulation amplitude varies linearly with the amplitude of the modulating LF signal. It is characteristic of the multiplicative system that if the modulating signal is sinusoidal, a purely sinusoidal modulation with only two side frequencies will result.

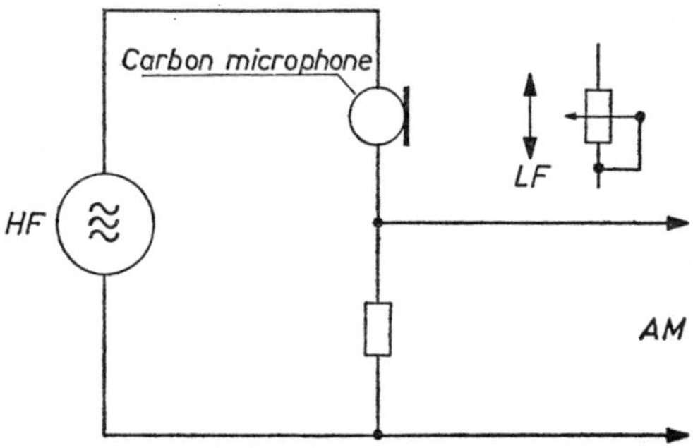

Fig. 3.18. Multiplicative modulation with a microphone

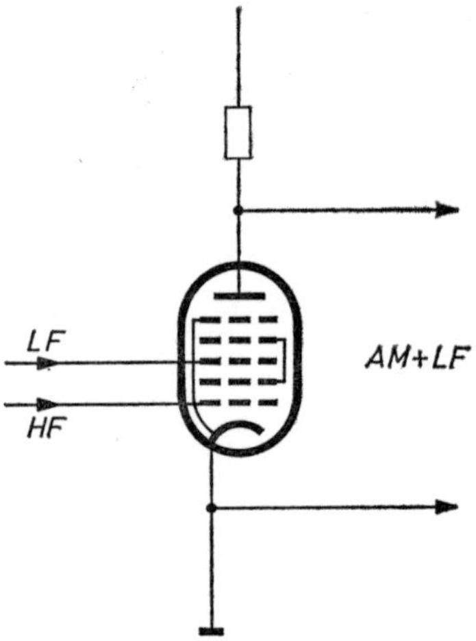

Fig. 3.19. Multiplicative modulation by controlling two grids of a heptode

This type of amplitude modulation must not be confused with methods having a non-linear characteristic, which in addition to the two above-mentioned side frequencies always involve higher-order side frequencies.

Amplitude modulation in which a circuit having non-linear characteristics is made to oscillate, is also referred to as additive mixing, and can take place in the grid-anode path of an electron tube simply by means of a diode. There will then be a whole series of mixing products so that in contrast with multiplicative modulation there will then be more side frequencies each formed by multiples of the modulation frequency. Pure amplitude modulation with no more than two side frequencies is only obtained by filtering out the pure AM components by means of a resonance circuit of the appropriate bandwidth. In radio receiver practice, additive mixing of a received frequency and local oscillator frequency also results in an intermediate frequency, one sideband of which is filtered out. This is illustrated by Fig. 3.20 showing a part of the circuit diagram of a radio receiver. Here the two signals are either added in the grid-cathode path of an electron tube or at the base-emitter circuit of a transistor (see Fig. 3.20).

3.3.3 Amplitude modulation with suppressed carrier

Since in amplitude modulation no d.c. components are transmitted, the LF information is contained only in the side bands. The carrier amplitude

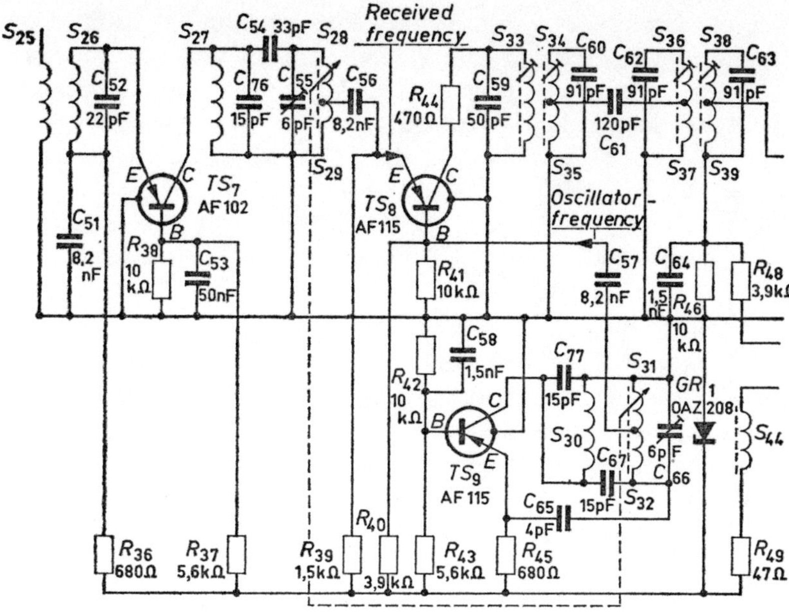

Fig. 3.20. Circuit diagram to explain additive mixing

does not vary, so that the carrier plays no part in transmitting LF information, and is required at the receiving end only for the purpose of demodulation. Amplitude modulation can easily be produced by means of a modulator circuit as shown in Fig. 3.21.

Diodes GR_1 to GR_4, connected with the polarity indicated, establish the connection between transformers T_1 and T_2. At the correct polarity of the HF signal fed to the electrical centre of the transformers, diodes GR_1 and GR_2 are conductive. Consequently the transformers are connected direct

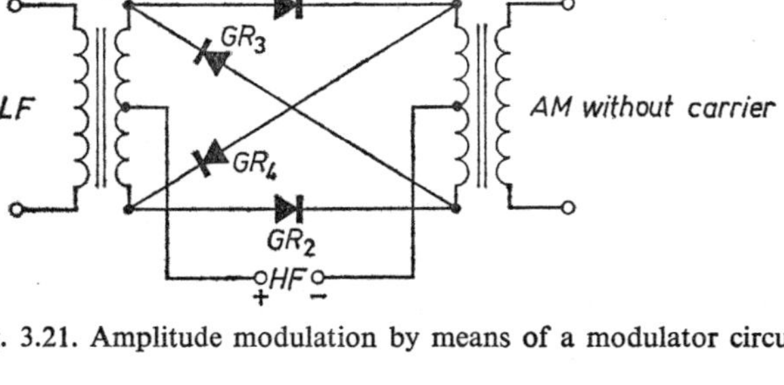

Fig. 3.21. Amplitude modulation by means of a modulator circuit

with each other in such a way that the LF signal is available at the output of transformer T_2. When, during the following half cycle, the polarity of the HF signal is reversed, diodes GR_1 and GR_2 are blocked, and diodes GR_3 and GR_4 are now conductive. The connection between the two transformers is now reversed. As the polarity of the HF signal reverses constantly, an LF signal whose polarity changes at the same frequency becomes available at the output of the transformer T_2. The HF signal will have no effect on the output of transformer T_2 as the supply to the centre tapping of one winding of the transformer ensures that the two half windings are in opposition so that no secondary HF voltage is induced.

If a 38 kc/s HF signal and a 4.22 kc/s signal are fed to the modulator of Fig. 3.21, the output of transformer T_2 will follow the gradient of the difference signal ($L - R$) shown in Fig. 3.14. As already mentioned, the resemblance between the form of the difference signal and the form of amplitude modulation with suppressed carrier is at once recognised (see Section 3.3.1). For the sake of clarity this is illustrated once more by Fig. 3.22.

In Fig. 3.22 the envelope of the amplitude, crossing zero, represents the difference signal ($L - R$) changing polarity at a frequency of 38 kc/s. This 38 kc/s voltage is obviously produced by the stereo signal. It can also be obtained by means of a modulator circuit. The actual carrier frequency of 38 kc/s is clearly not available in the modulator although the output voltage oscillates at a frequency of 38 kc/s.

But how do we know that the output voltage of the modulator contains no 38 kc/s component? The answer lies in the phase shift occurring at the cross-over point of the envelope. When changing over from one zero-crossing envelope to another — when the modulator switches over, i.e. when the stereo signal is produced (see Section 3.2.2) — the positive 39 kc/s voltage approaches zero (see Fig. 3.22) but does not become negative. It seems to remain positive after having undergone a phase shift of exactly 180°. If we now try to filter a 38 kc/s component out of the ($L - R$) difference signal —

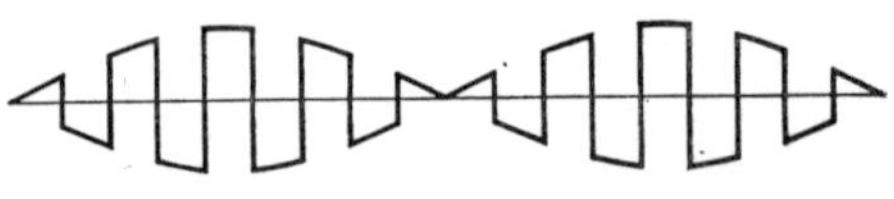

Fig. 3.22. The form of amplitude modulation with suppressed carrier resembles the gradient of the difference signal

as compared with the carrier amplitude — by using a resonant circuit tuned to 38 kc/s, we find that the mean value is zero. This is because the resonant circuit is counter-excited by the phase reversal and consequently no oscillation whatsoever will occur over several periods. Therefore the difference signal contains no 38 kc/s component. The 38 kc/s voltage, resembling an AM oscillation with suppressed carrier, contains only the side frequencies 38 kc/s $+ f_{(L-R)}$ and 38 kc/s $- f_{(L-R)}$, which can easily be checked by experiment. These effects are analogous to those in the example given in Section 3.3.1 by means of the circuit shown in Fig. 3.15.

Finally it may be noted that a ring modulator circuit gives amplitude modulation with suppressed carrier. This type of amplitude modulation is characterised by the occurrence of phase inversion and the fact that the modulation curve crosses the zero line while the ring modulator only switches over. The 38 kc/s oscillation of the difference signal $(L - R)$ represents an amplitude modulation with suppressed carrier, and the side frequencies of 38 kc/s $+ f_{(L-R)}$ and 38 kc/s $- f_{(L-R)}$.

CHAPTER 4

STEREOPHONIC RADIO TRANSMISSION

The preceding chapter showed how a stereo signal is obtained by the change-over method (see Section 3.2 and Fig. 3.3). Another method is the matrix method which also supplies a sum and difference signal [40]. Just as the stereo signal can be divided into a sum and difference signal, so can it be formed by adding the two signals. This can also be done without a continuous changing-over of L and R as is briefly explained below.

The sum signal $(L + R)$ and the difference signal $(L - R)$ can be obtained by connecting the microphones for L and R appropriately to a so-called matrix. The LF difference signal must now be superimposed on the 38 kc/s voltage (see Section 3.3.1). This added to the LF sum signal gives the stereo signal. At first sight this matrix system seems complicated. But it has one great advantage which should not be overlooked. That is the fact that at the receiving end the amplitude of the difference signal which, as we know, contains directional information, can be adjusted at will. This makes reception more flexible. A greater amplitude of the difference signal gives a better impression of space; the sound waves seem to spread out like a fan, and for that reason are often referred to as a stereo fan.

For the sake of clarity such a matrix circuit is shown in Fig. 4.1. After amplification the L information is fed to transformer T_1. The R information is likewise fed to transformer T_2. S_2 and S_3 of the secondary windings of the transformers are connected in series and their outputs reinforce each other; they supply the sum signal $(L + R)$. S_1 and S_4 are connected in phase opposition and their outputs oppose each other; they supply the difference signal $(L - R)$. After amplification of the difference signal its amplitude can be adjusted to produce the stereo fan effect. In a modulator (see Section 3.3.1) the LF difference signal is superimposed on the 38 kc/s signal. The result of this is now added to the sum signal, making the stereo signal proper available across output resistor R_A. This signal is the same as the one obtained according to the change-over method, the only difference being that now the difference signal can be adjusted to form the stereo fan.

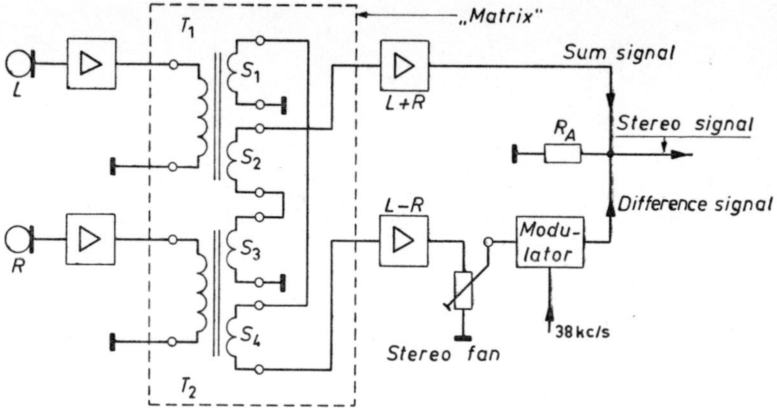

Fig. 4.1. Matrix circuit to produce the sum and difference signal.

As already explained the frequency spectrum of the stereo signal extends as far as 53 kc/s (see Section 3.2.4). It can be broadcast by USW-FM transmitters. Although the following chapters will not deal with the circuitry of stereo transmitters, there are however a few points which may be of interest from the receiving point of view [40].

4.1 Intensity stereophony

Stereophony in the sense discussed here is based on the transmission and reproduction of two sound signals as comparatively perceived by the human ear (see Section 1.1). This can be done, for example ,by means of two microphones mounted at appropriate positions in a dummy head thus representing the human ears (see Section 1.3). This method of perceiving sound involves differences between the *L* and *R* information as regards amplitude, phase, and sound colour. Experience has shown, however, that a satisfactory stereo effect can also be produced in recording and transmission without necessarily using all three of the above-mentioned characteristics.

A distinct amplitude difference already gives a good stereo impression. Such 'intensity' stereophony has the advantage that in the sum signal, also called the mono signal, no frequencies can be blanked out and thus lost owing to phase opposition when phase shift occurs. This is a condition which is very important as regards compatibility (see Section 3.2.5). With intensity stereophony use is made of two microphones mounted at the same point. There are then no differences in phase and sound colour. The microphones used have distinct directional response (see Section 2.1); this can be a cardioid response, for instance, as shown in Fig. 4.2. The microphones are so mounted that the axes of their directional characteristics are at an angle of 120° with each other. The percentage amplitudes given in Fig. 4.2 only apply to the special case in which the sound source describes part of a circle with the microphones at the centre. The values correspond to the directions —60°, —30°, 0°, 30° and 60°. The amplitude modulation of the transmitter is also given for each of these directions.

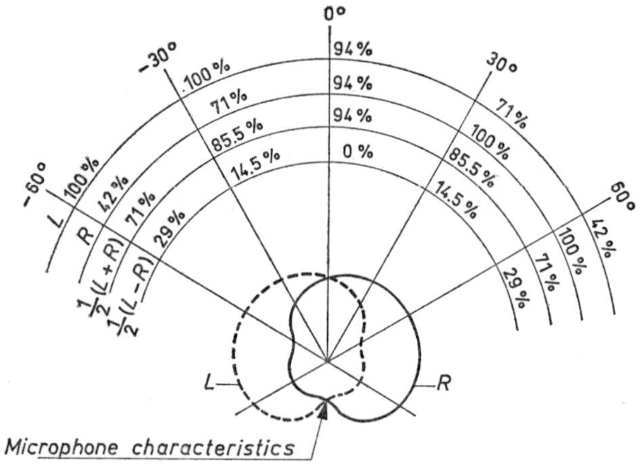

Fig. 4.2. Principle of intensity stereophony

4.2 Transmitter control

For transmitter control it is a requirement that the amplitude of the pilot tone should be 10 % of the maximum modulation depth. The remaining 90 % is then available for the stereo signal (see Section 3.2.4). For the two cardioid microphones used in the preceding example, the transmitter control will now be determined for two directions. The starting point will be a frequency band from 30 c/s to 15 kc/s.

4.2.1 0° direction

The 0° direction is the acoustic centre line. In this case the microphones give equal amplitudes. According to the directional response characteristics of the microphones the maximum amplitude is $L = R = 94\%$ (see Section 4.2). The amplitude of the sum signal $(L + R)$ is also 94%, while the amplitude of the difference signal $(L - R)$ is zero. This leads to the conclusion that the 'acoustic-centre' signal is at the same time a pure mono signal. Fig. 4.3 shows a diagram representing transmitter modulation for 0° direction. At an 'acoustic-centre' signal the stereo transmitter is modulated practically like a mono transmitter, that is to say with the sum signal. This indicates an amplitude of 94%. Taking a 10% pilot tone modulation into account, a depth of 90% is available for maximum amplitude of the sum signal; the actual modulation depth in this case will therefore be $90 \times 0.94 = 84.6\%$ and the total transmitter modulation is then $84.6 + 10 = 94.6\%$.

4.2.2 —60° direction

According to Fig. 4.2 the amplitudes for L and R are 100% and 42% respectively. The amplitude of the sum signal $(L + R)$ is 70%, and that of the difference signal 29%. The latter is equally divided over the two side bands each part being 14.5%. For a maximum useful 90% modulation of the carrier these values must be multiplied by 0.9. The diagram of the transmitter modulation, see Fig. 4.4, concerns the direction —60°.

From the diagrams in Fig. 4.3 and 4.4 it follows that the amplitude of the sum signal, also called the mono signal where mono receivers are considered, becomes 63.9% instead of 84.6% as found for the 0° direction. For purely monophonic operation the transmitter would have been modulated to full 100% for any direction. It is therefore seen that, if only intensity stereophony is used, the average amplitude of the mono signal in a stereo trans-

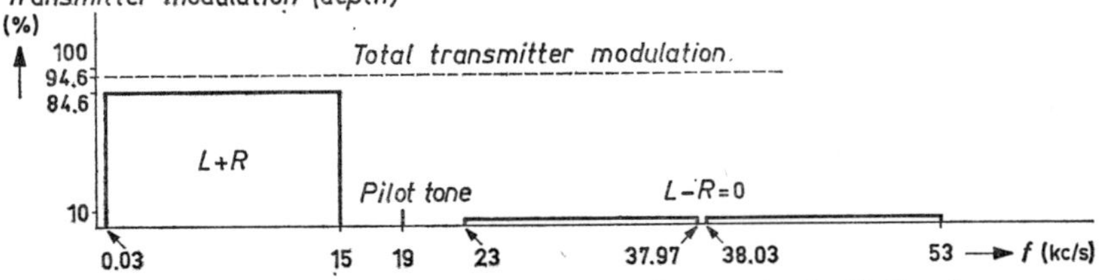

Fig. 4.3. Transmitter modulation for a sound source in the 0° direction

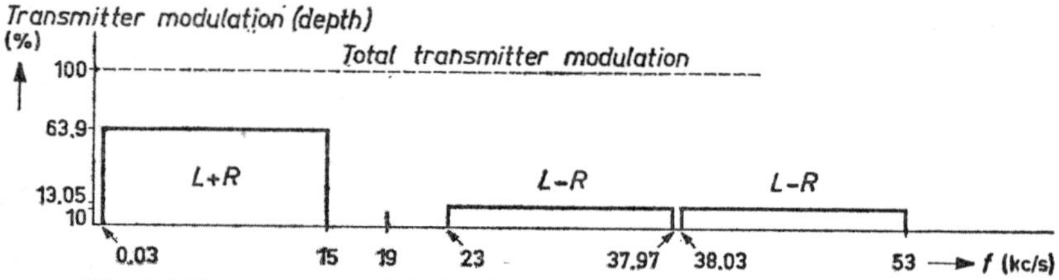

Fig. 4.4. Transmitter modulation for a sound source in the —60° direction

mitter is no more than about 70% of the radiation by a mono transmitter. The actual values obtained are, however, better (see Section 3.2.4).

4.3 Transmitter bandwidth

With frequency modulation the number of side frequencies, and consequently the transmission bandwidth B, depends on the maximum frequency amplitude $\Delta f_{HF\ \max}$ and the corresponding highest modulation frequency $f_{LF\ \max}$. Expressed in a formula:

$$B_{\max} = 2\,(\Delta f_{HF\ \max} + 2 f_{LF\ \max}).$$

For a maximum modulation frequency $f_{LF\ \max} = 15$ kc/s and a corresponding maximum frequency depth $\Delta f_{LHF\ \max} = 75$ k/s this yields a maximum bandwidth $B_{\max} = 210$ kc/s for FM transmission — hence the channel separation of 300 kc/s which must be observed. As however, maximum modulation for a stereo signal is $f_{LF} =_{\max} 53$ kc/s, bandwidth B is automatically increased. To work out the formula given above, the maximum frequency sweep $\Delta f_{HF\ \max}$ must be known. The bandwidth occupied by the difference signal will be maximum when one of the L or R signals is missing, that is to say, if one of these amplitudes is zero. For in that case the difference signal will be maximum. If $L = 100\%$ and $R = 0\%$ we have the situation shown in Fig. 4.5. This is the border case of maximum transmission bandwidth. One side band is then modulated 22.5%. The maximum frequency $f_{LF\ \max} =$ 53 kc/s gives a frequency modulation of $\Delta f_{HF} = 75 \times 0.225 = 16.9$ kc/s. By means of this corresponding frequency modulation the maximum bandwidth can be found from the formula given above:

$$B_{\max} = 2\,(\Delta f_{HF\ \max} + 3 f_{LF\ \max}) = 2\,[16.9 + (2 \times 53)] = 246 \text{ kc/s}.$$

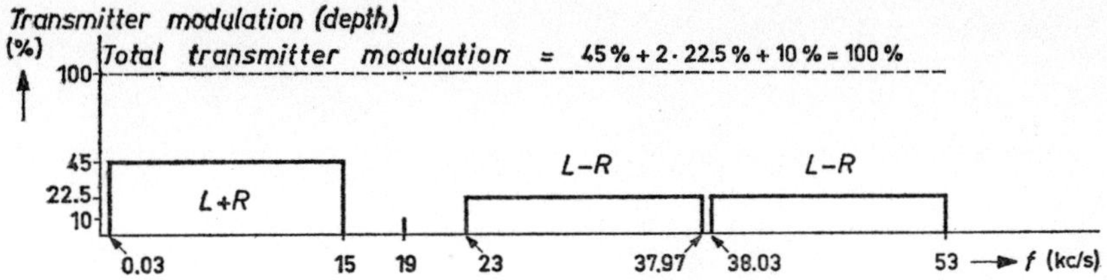

Fig. 4.5. Transmitter modulation without *R* signal

This clearly indicates that stereo transmission involves a bandwidth which is wider by a factor 1.2 than that of mono transmission so that the channel separation of 300 kc/s is never exceeded.

CHAPTER 5

STEREOPHONIC RECEPTION

From what has been said in the preceding sections it will be obvious that the IF amplifier as well as the ratio detector in a stereo receiver will have to satisfy more stringent demands than those for a mono receiver. The reason for this lies in the larger frequency content of the stereo signal. As already stated in Section 4.3, the maximum bandwidth for stereo transmissions is 246 kc/s. This value is only reached momentarily when the greatest sound volume is being transmitted. The corresponding value for mono transmission is 210 kc/s. Although the effects on the IF amplifier are not serious, they are present. Experience has shown that an IF bandwidth of 180—200 kc/s is sufficient for stereo receivers; for mono receivers it is even less. And herein lies one of the reasons why older types of radio sets afterwards modified for HF stereophony are unsatisfactory.

Transmission of higher modulation frequencies introduces a growing risk that the stereo signal may be distorted in the IF amplifier due to various phase shifts, thus causing unacceptable crosstalk and increased harmonic distortion [40].

As the stereo signal produced at the output of the ratio detector can contain frequencies up to 53 kc/s, there must be a significantly higher LF limit for the ratio detector than for the monophonic system (see Section 3.2.4).

Considering that the two LF signals (L and R) are combined in the transmitter in which they are coded, it can be logically concluded that they can be separated again in the receiver if they are appropriately decoded. This is done in what is called a stereo decoder which has the following three functions:

1. Restoring the 38 kc/s carrier
2. Forming the L and R signal by combining the main channel and secondary channel
3. De-emphasis.

Development of such decoder circuits presents a variety of rather complex problems. It is not surprising, therefore, that a correspondingly large number of solutions have been found. Not only are there several different decoding systems, but different circuitry can be used for one and the same system [42]. There are actually three principles upon which decoders can be based: the switch decoder, the envelope decoder and the matrix decoder. These are discussed in the first three sections of this chapter [40] followed by a section devoted to the indicating circuits employed in stereo reception.

5.1 Switch decoder

It has already been explained in Section 3.2 how, by means of two simultaneously operated switches, one in the transmitter and one in the receiver, which constantly interchange the *L* and *R* channel, stereo signals can be broadcast using one transmitter only. Of course, using a mechanical switch for this purpose is out of the question, since the switching frequency is 38 kc/s! Consequently switching must be done electronically.

It is seen from the block diagram in Fig. 5.1 that the first component following the ratio detector is a low-pass filter with a limit frequency of 55 kc/s so that it will allow the total stereo signal to pass. A 38 kc/s voltage is required for the synchronous switching of the two channels. This is obtained by first filtering out the 19 kc/s pilot tone of the stereo signal, and then doubling its frequency. The 38 kc/s voltage thus obtained is used to drive two counter-phase electronic switches to which the complete stereo signal is applied. When operating at the correct phase, accurate 38 kc/s switching takes place at the right moment so that the two channels are separated from each other.

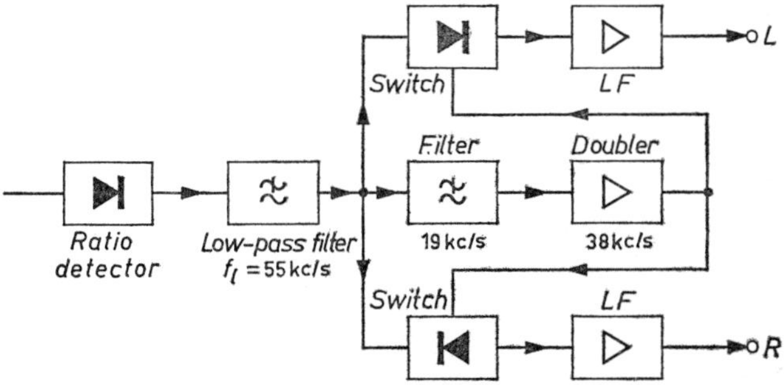

Fig. 5.1. Block diagram of the switch decoder

Even with the best designed and adjusted switching arrangement, however, it is impossible to separate the channels completely, and therefore use is made of what is known as cross-talk compensation. Its principle is briefly as follows. To begin with Fig. 5.2 shows a stereo signal without pilot tone and only one channel ($R = 0$). In the transmitter repeated switching therefore takes place between the L channel and zero. This results in very steep signal flanks which can only be transmitted as such if the bandwidth of 53 kc/s is exceeded. However, as even before modulation all frequencies exceeding 53 kc/s are suppressed, obliquely distorted sinusoidal flanks only are transmitted. If the decoder now switches over from the L channel to the R channel ($R = 0$), the residual signal of the L channel will still be present (shaded area).

Fig. 5.3a again shows the stereo signal with its oblique flank. The pulses produced in the L channel of the decoder due to the 38 kc/s switching operation are shown in Fig. 5.3b. After de-emphasis the r.m.s. value of the signal follows the broken line in the graph, which represents the useful LF signal. Fig. 5.3c clearly shows the residual signal, or rather the spurious signal in the R channel ($R = 0$) when switching takes place at the correct phase. It is thus seen that notwithstanding a complete lack of R modulation in the transmitter, a signal actually derived from the L channel appears in the decoder. This signal is formed by the oblique flanks in the L channel and can be considered as a form of cross-talk.

If no cross-talk compensation were used, the de-emphasis filter would also produce a useful LF signal as indicated by the broken curve in Fig. 5.3c, so that a signal of the same frequency as that in the modulated L channel would be produced in the R channel (see Fig. 5.3d). To avoid this, the phase of the signal components of the modulated channel is reversed in the decoder, and the inverted signal is fed to the unmodulated channel. This is illustrated

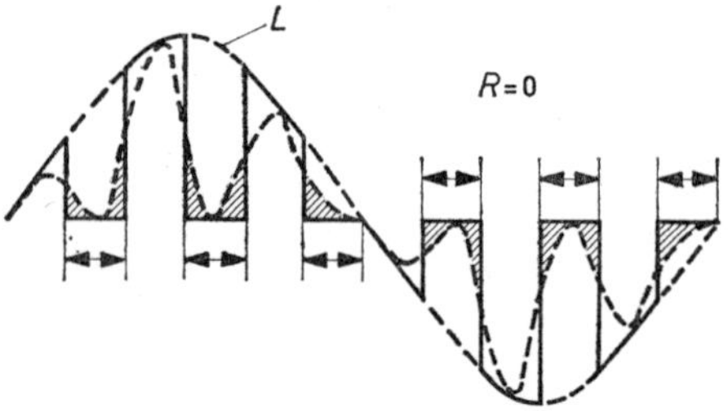

Fig. 5.2. Stereo signal without pilot tone and with only one channel ($R = 0$)

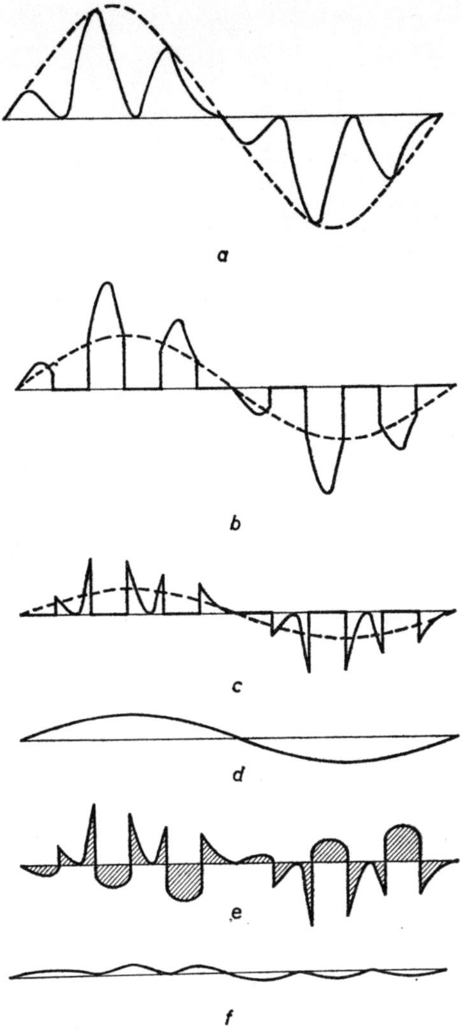

Fig. 5.3. Various stages of the stereo signal as fed to the cross-talk compensator. Explanations are given in the text

in Fig. 5.3c. If the areas enclosed by the curves, both in the negative and positive sense, are made practically equal by appropriate adjustment of the compensation voltage, cross-talk will be reduced to a minimum. When the 38 kc/s signal is filtered out, the most favourable condition will occur at the instant at which the resulting average value coincides with the zero line. It will be clear, however, that the areas enclosed by the curve will not be absolutely equal owing to a certain amount of asymmetry. Consequently there will always be a certain amount of cross-talk as is shown in Fig. 5.3f. It should be borne in mind that this compensation method is not based on the principle of two equal signals in phase opposition thus neutralising each other. This would, of course, ensure that the resultant value would be zero which would mean perfect compensation. As it is, cross-talk is rather compensated by the mean value of voltages in phase opposition.

Fig. 5.4 gives the circuit diagram of a switch decoder used in practice [43]. The input of the decoder is connected to the ratio detector. The resonant circuit consisting of coil S_{101} is tuned to the frequency of the pilot tone (19 kc/s). After having passed this filter the pilot tone is fed to the base of transistor TS_{201}. The transducer included in the collector circuit of this transistor is also tuned to 19 kc/s. The amplified pilot tone appears at the secondary winding consisting of coils S_{105} and S_{106}, whose centre tap is connected to earth. The frequency of the pilot tone is doubled to 38 kc/s in the full wave rectifier consisting of diodes GR_{201} and GR_{202}. This frequency is applied across load resistor R_{205} and is amplified by transistor TS_{202}. In the collector circuit of transistor TS_{202} this frequency is fed through a filter consisting of coil S_{107} and capacitor C_{209}. It is then fed via secondary winding S_{108}/S_{109} to the demodulator consisting of diodes GR_{203}, GR_{204}, GR_{205} and GR_{206}. Via a parallel connection S_{103} and capacitor C_{205} blocking the SCA signal (see Section 3.2.1), the stereo signal is applied to the centre tap of the secondary winding consisting of coils S_{108} and S_{109}. The regener-

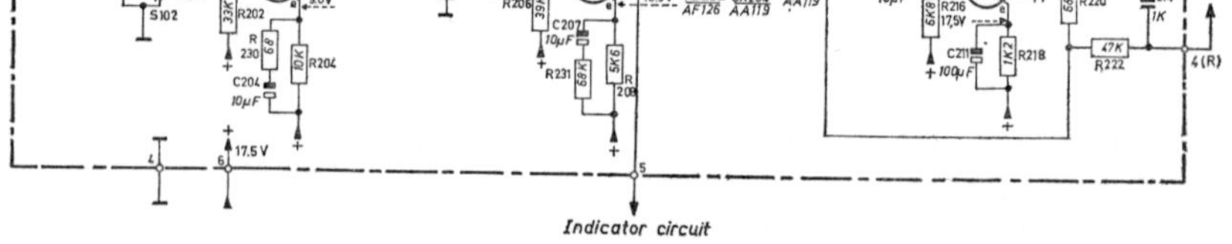

Fig. 5.4. Circuit diagram of a switch decoder as used in practice

ated subcarrier is now demodulated. Together with the sum signal it makes the L information available at point Y (junction of $R_{210}/GR_{203}/R_{215}$), and the R information at point Z (junction of $R_{211}/GR_{205}/R_{214}$). Both L and R information are fed to the two LF amplifier channels via de-emphasis circuits R_{223}/C_{213} and R_{222}/C_{214} respectively.

The final stage with transistor TS_{203} serves to compensate cross-talk. If at a given instant the R channel is switched on, a part of the R signal will arrive at the base of transistor TS_{203} via voltage divider R_{213}—R_{214}. After amplification this part of the signal appears at the collector in counter phase and is fed to the left channel via resistor R_{221}. This is in accordance with the explanation given with Fig. 5.3e. By adjusting the cross-talk compensation with variable resistor R_{213}, cross-talk can be kept at minimum. If at the next instant the L channel is switched on, a part of the L signal will reach the base of transistor TS_{203} via voltage divider R_{213}-R_{215}. After amplification this counter phase signal in turn is fed into the R channel via resistor R_{220}. The part of the signal thus led back to its own channel has hardly any effect on the output amplitude. As the current supply for the decoder is derived from the operating voltage of the valve receiver, the negative terminal of the circuit is connected to earth.

5.2 Envelope decoder

This decoder is also based on the principle of adding a 38 kc/s signal u_I to the stereo signal (Fig. 5.5a). As a result the two envelopes are separated (Fig. 5.5b) [41]. The minimum components needed to achieve this are two diodes with corresponding RC circuits and a suitable network for combining the stereo signal and the subcarrier [42]. The block diagram is given in Fig. 5.6; the corresponding practical wiring diagram is shown in Fig. 5.7.

To be able to cope with voltages of up to 7 V, feed-back is applied to the first stage with transistor TS_1 via a relatively large emitter resistor R_4. At the same time this provides an input impedance of at least 100 kΩ. The amplified pilot frequency (19 kc/s) is available at the collector of transistor TS_1. Owing to the input impedance which must also be high at 19 kc/s a suction circuit cannot be used in this first stage. Instead an HF transistor type A127 with a sufficiently low reactance is used. Now the input impedance of the decoder remains sufficiently high at 19 kc/s although the relatively high oscillator voltages are applied to the collector of transistor TS_1. The second

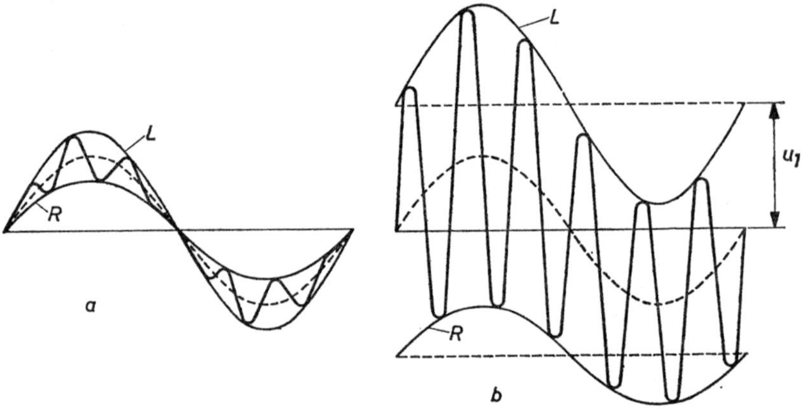

Fig. 5.5. Principle of the envelope decoder; a constant 38 kc/s signal is added to the stereo signal (a) so that the two envelopes are forced apart (b)

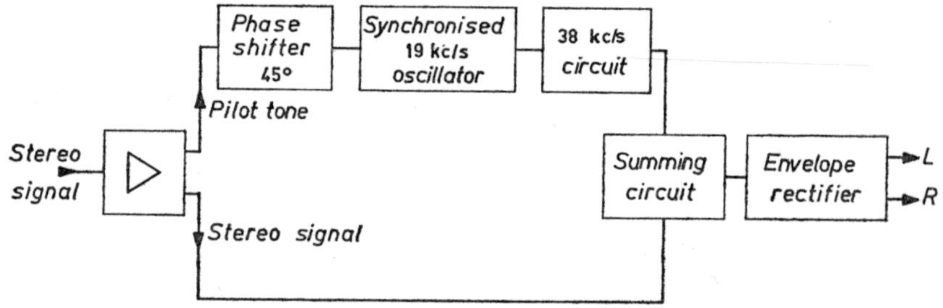

Fig. 5.6. Block diagram of envelope decoder

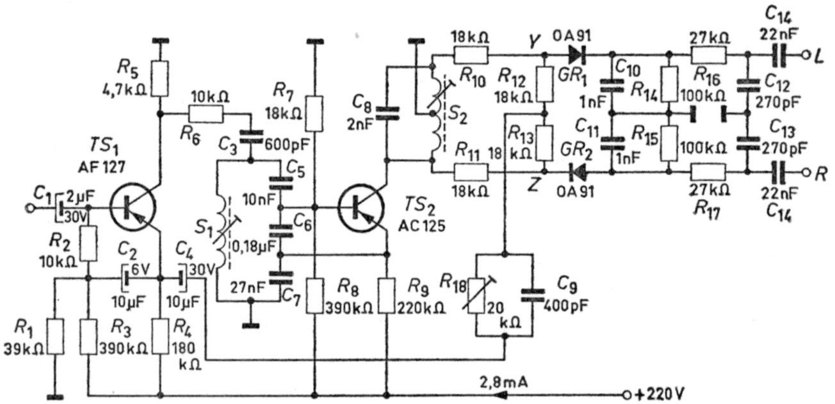

Fig. 5.7. Practical circuit diagram of an envelope decoder

stage with transistor TS_2 functions as a 19 kc/s oscillator which is synchronised by the pilot tone. Capacitors C_5 and C_1 provide voltage division required for the feedback. The circuit consisting of resistor R_6 and capacitor C_3 is so dimensioned that the 45° phase shift between the pilot tone and the input, and the voltage at the resonant circuit remains quite independent of the amplitude of the pilot tone. This also ensures satisfactory synchronisation up to a pilot tone amplitude of 50 mV. The operating point of the second stage is so chosen that modulation by the pilot tone takes place in the least linear part of the characteristic. As a result the collector current of transistor TS_2 is distorted. In the 38 kc/s resonant circuit consisting of S_2 and C_8 this distorted current generates a carrier amplitude of about 8.5 V. Any feedback of 38 kc/s components and their harmonics to the input is entirely prevented by making the 38 kc/s resonance circuit and also the bridge formed by the summing circuit asymmetrical. The L signal appears at point Y (junction $R_{10}/GR_1/R_{12}$), the R signal appears at point Z (junction $R_{11}/GR_2/R_{13}$), that is to say as the positive and negative envelopes respectively. Diodes GR_1 and GR_2 form the point-contact rectifier for the envelope formed by the addition of subcarrier and stereo signal.

This decoding method too, involves cross-talk. Compensation can be obtained by removing the high frequencies of the difference signal by means of a high-pass *RC* filter. In Fig. 5.7 this filter consists of resistor R_{18} and capacitor C_9. Cross-talk is minimised by appropriate adjustment of resistor R_{18}. In this circuit too, the negative pole is connected to earth, as the current supply for the decoder is obtained from the operating voltage of the valve-operated receiver.

5.3 Matrix decoder

The action of this decoder is the reverse of that of the matrix system explained in connection with Fig. 4.1, which produces the stereo 'fan' at the transmitter. The block diagram is shown in Fig. 5.8 [40, 41]. Just as the sum signal $(L + R)$ and the difference signal $(L — R)$ can be combined at the transmitter to form the stereo signal, they can be separated again at the receiver. The sum signal $(L + R)$ is recovered by means of a low-pass filter (0 — 15 kc/s). The difference signal $(L — R)$ is restored via a bandpass filter (23 — 53 kc/s). Paying due attention to phase relationship, the suppressed 38 kc/s carrier can be added again after the pilot tone (19 kc/s) has been

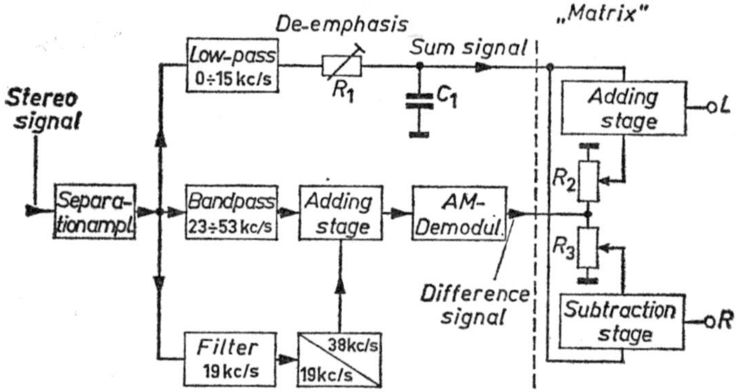

Fig. 5.8. Block diagram of the matrix decoder

doubled. The resulting amplitude-modulated oscillations can than be demodulated in the usual way with a diode. Addition of the sum and difference signal gives the *L* signal, subtraction of the two gives the *R* signal.

As regards cross-talk it may be said that in both the above-mentioned systems (see Section 5.1) oblique interfering flanks produce no undesirable effect. They originate from the maximum frequency of the difference-signal channel corresponding to the transmitted bandwidth. If the sum and difference signals could indeed be recovered without any amplitude or phase distortion, perfect channel separation would be ensured. However, the two signals travel along different paths so that with this method also ideal separation of the two channels cannot be achieved. For each of the two channels cross-talk is separately damped by varying the amplitude of the difference signal fed to the integrating or differentiating stage respectively. The variable resistors used for these adjustments are indicated in the block diagram of Fig. 5.8 as R_2 and R_3 respectively. The frequency response of the sum-signal channel can be varied by means of resistor R_1 of de-emphasis circuit R_1/C_1 so that cross-talk at different frequencies can be reduced to a minimum. It has been found that matrix decoders offer no advantage over switching decoders, either as regards channel separation or cost.

5.4 Indicator circuits

The introduction of decoders for stereo reception has been accompanied by the use of indicator circuits, the function of which is to inform the listener whether the selected station is transmitting a stereo signal. There are two types of indicator circuits, one making use of the familiar 'magic eye', and the other employing small incandescent lamps. There are obvious reasons which dictate what system should be chosen for a particular receiver. If the radio set is already equipped with electron tubes, there is no reason, either from the electrical or the optical point of view why an extra stereo indicator tube should not be used. In a transistor radio, however, miniature incandescent lamps are usually more suitable, as they operate on the same current supply as the transistors.

Fig. 5.9 shows an indicator circuit operating with a tuning indicator tube EM 87. The doubled pilot tone frequency (38 kc/s) serves as the control signal. This signal is produced by the switch decoder shown in Fig. 5.4, and is applied to the collector of transistor TS_2. The resonant circuit formed by coil S_{48} and capacitor C_{100} is tuned to 38 kc/s. The amplified 38 kc/s voltage is rectified by diode Gr_{10} and is fed back to the control grid of the indicator tube whose triode system also functions as a d.c. amplifier. The voltage produced at the anode serves to drive the indicator system [44].

from decoder

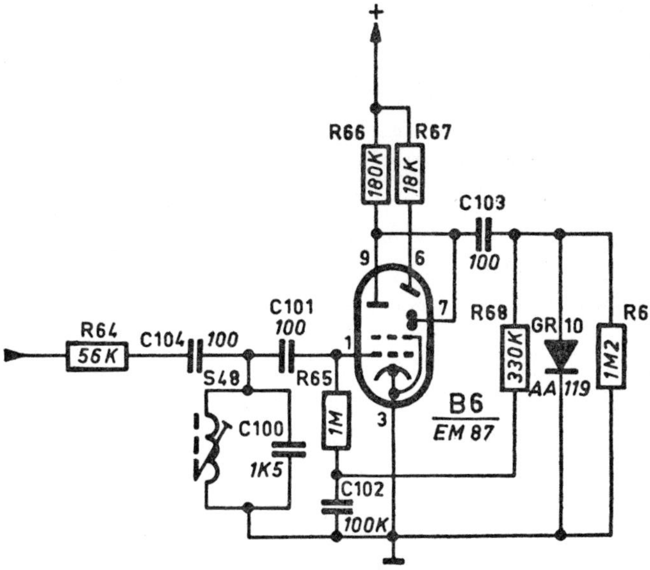

Fig. 5.9. Indicator circuit with a tuning indicator tube EM 87

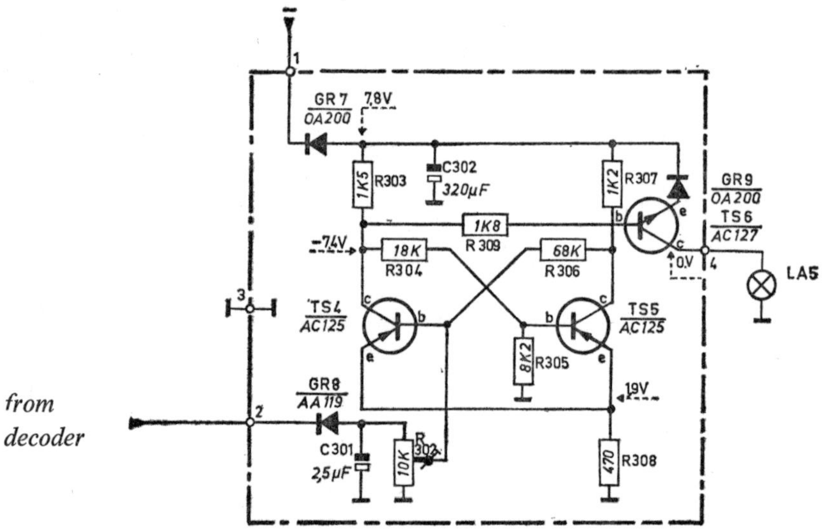

Fig. 5.10. Indicator circuit using a miniature incandescent lamp

Fig. 5.10 shows an indicator circuit in which a miniature incandescent lamp is used as the indicator. In this case too, the pilot tone frequency doubled to 38 kc/s serves as the control signal. Again the signal is produced by the switching decoder illustrated in Fig. 5.4. In contrast with the indicator circuit of Fig. 5.9, however, there is no resonant circuit, but a discriminator is used instead. This circuit is connected to transistor TS_{202} of the decoder via diode GR_8. The threshold can be adjusted by means of variable resistor R_{302}. Transistors TS_4 and TS_5 form the discriminator which in turn drives an indicator amplifier containing transistor TS_6, in the collector circuit of which pilot lamp LA_5 is connected. [43]

In either case the deflection of the indicator tube or the light intensity of the pilot lamp not only provides an indication of a stereo signal. The risk of greater interference which exists at lower field strengths can also be inferred from weak deflections or a flickering pilot lamp.

CHAPTER 6

TESTING LF STEREOPHONY PLAYBACK EQUIPMENT

This chapter is not intended to give a detailed description of testing playback equipment. In the first place to do so would require more space then is available in the book; and furthermore, adequate special literature is already available on the subject [45]. However a few important points in stereo reproduction will be discussed here, while others will be mentioned more briefly in passing. The following sections of this chapter will deal with record players, tape recorders, amplifiers and loudspeakers successively.

6.1 Record players

It goes without saying that when testing record players the technician should also check the speed of the turn-table. Unfortunately, however, this point, which is at least equally important for stereo records as it is for mono records, usually receives no attention 'There can be nothing wrong with that,' has often been said by persons who later have wondered why records, and especially piano records, made such a wailing sound when played. The speed of the record player can easily be checked with the stroboscopic disc usually presented free of charge by the manufacturer. Fig. 6.1 shows a typical stroboscopic disc printed with circles of stripes for indicating positive and negative errors for each speed. The disc must be illuminated from the most constant light source available; discharge lamps and fluorescent lamps are the most suitable. If no such lamp is available an incandescent lamp can be used. A first requirement is, however, that the mains to which the lamp is connected are not subject to frequency fluctuations. Directions for adjusting the speed of the various types of record players and automatic record changer can be obtained from the dealers. Another important item is the playback head. The technician can easily tell whether a crystal system has reached the end of its working life, for a worn crystal does not only give distorted sound reproduction, but also supplies too low an output voltage. These are faults

Fig. 6.1. Stroboscopic disc to check the speed of record players

that can be heard without any special aid. In this connection the condition of the stylus is particularly important [13]. The fact cannot be stressed enough that the stylus is particularly liable to wear, so that in due course it must regularly be replaced by a new one.

The material of which the stylus is made is usually sapphire or diamond. The shape is always the same; a round stem about 0.4 mm thick and about 1 mm long the end being a rounded-off cone (angle 45°). The forms and dimensions of the roundings (see table 2.4) correspond to the various types of grooves. Fig. 6.2 shows an enlarged microgroove stylus. The different positions the stylus may take up in a groove have already been described in Section 2.2 and shown in the diagrams of Fig. 2.13. Worn needles are nothing more or less than 'groove wreckers'. A good impression of what

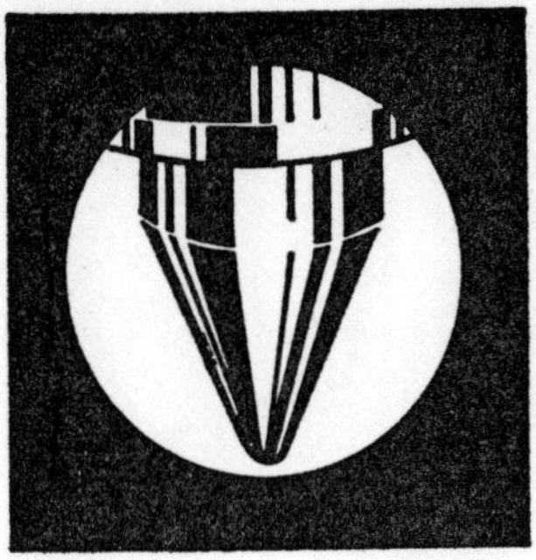

Fig. 6.2. Enlarged view of microgroove stylus

actually happens is given by Fig. 6.3. As the stylus becomes more and more worn the contact 'points' are ground off; they become contact planes. The stylus sinks deeper into the groove and slides over the bottom of the groove (Fig. 6.3a). The edges of the worn planes then drag along the walls of the groove thus causing serious damage where the groove is modulated deepest. Fig. 6.3b shows the position of the stylus in three different places of the groove. Once a stylus is worn to this extent, it soon wears out altogether. A badly-worn microgroove stylus is shown in Fig. 6.4, which should be compared with Fig. 6.2. The traces of wear shown in Fig. 6.4 are obvious. They are caused by excessive use. Distorted, bad sound reproduction and irreparable damage to the record are the inevitable results.

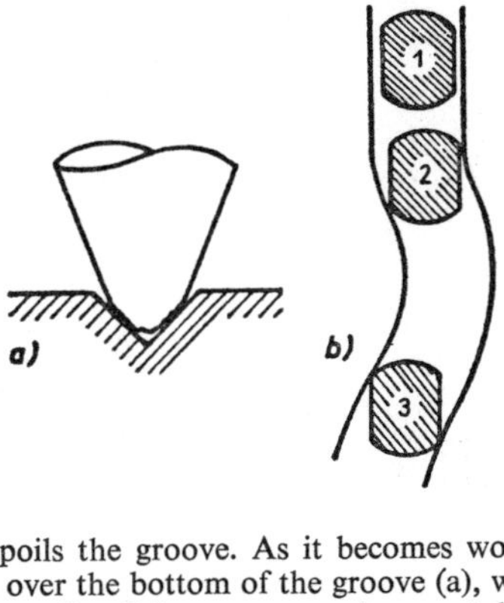

Fig. 6.3. A worn stylus spoils the groove. As it becomes worn the stylus sinks deeper into the groove and slides over the bottom of the groove (a), while the edges of the worn planes are drawn along the walls of the groove causing most damage where the groove is modulated deepest (b)

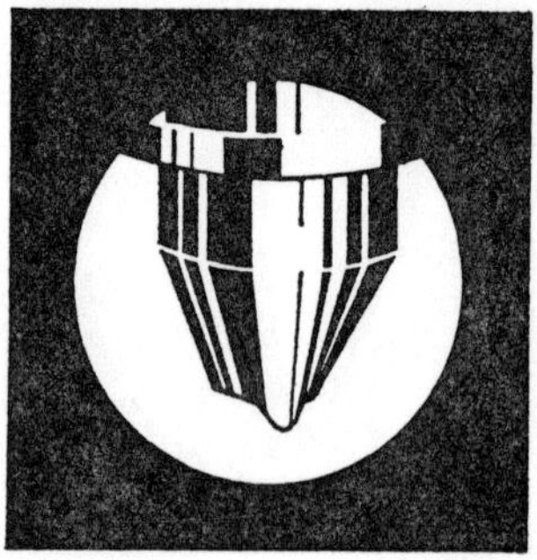

Fig. 6.4. Enlarged view of the microgroove stylus of Fig. 6.2; the effect of grinding is clearly visible

The effects described above are illustrated by the pictures of Fig. 6.5. Fig. 6.5a is a greatly enlarged picture of the sound groove of a new gramophone record and shows no change after having been played several times with a perfect stylus. In contrast, Fig. 6.5b shows the serious damage caused to the sound grooves by the sharp worn edges of the stylus. Such a record is spoiled for ever, and even the best playback equipment can no longer give good reproduction.

Unfortunately users generally become aware that reproduction heads or stylii are worn when it is already too late. The untrained ear hardly, if at all, perceives that the sound impression is beginning to deteriorate. Only then,

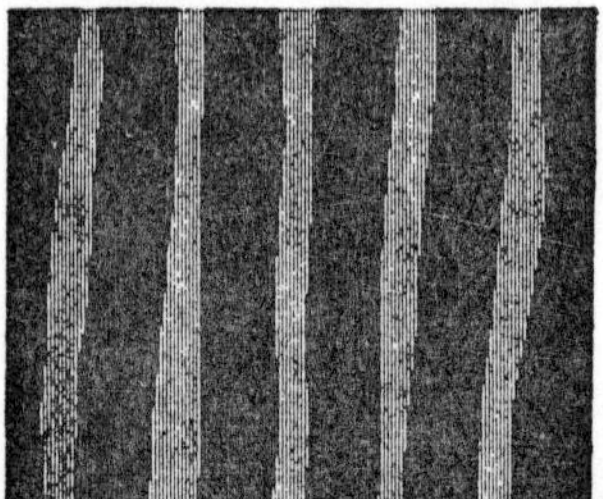

a

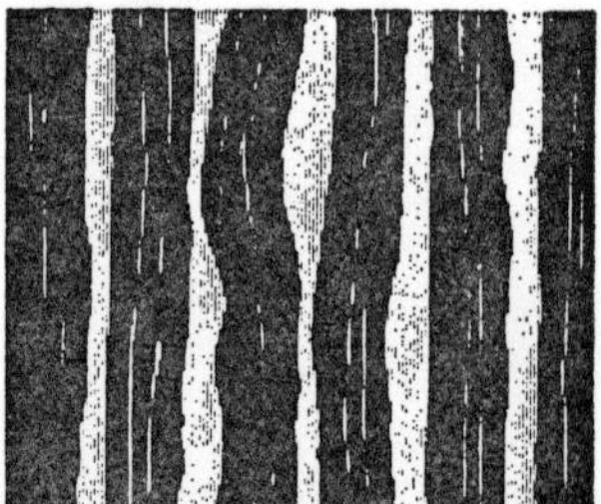

b

Fig. 6.5. Enlarged sound groove of a new record (a), and the same groove after having been mal-treated by a worn stylus (b) when matters have come to the point at which the reduction in quality can no longer be ignored is expert advice sought. Dealers and technicians should at the outset make it clear to users that a worn stylus must never be used.

It has been found from thorough investigation that a sapphire microgroove stylus can be used to play flawless records for about 125 hours before it needs replacing. Similar investigation carried out in the vicinity of workshops where metallic dust and other sharp particles are present indicated a 50-hour working life under the same conditions. Diamond stylii, however, have a much longer working life. The records played with diamond stylii showed considerably less wear; when treated in the right way they have an almost unlimited life-time.

The working life of stylii differs from case to case depending on the following factors:

1. Stylus material; a hard diamond stylus lasts about twice as long as the softer sapphire stylus.
2. Stylus pressure; too high a pressure accelerates wear. The pressure (weight) must always be adjusted in accordance with the instructions for the various types of equipment. Tone arms, whose pressure can be adjusted, should not be made too heavy for 'safety' reasons.
3. Condition of the records; scratched and dusty records cause a great deal of damage to the stylus. The types of dust most dangerous and also most difficult to remove are sharp sand and chalk particles and also the grindings of the sapphire itself. A slightly moist or specially prepared cloth can best be used to clean the records.
4. Tone arm; as it travels in the sound groove towards the centre of the record, the stylus always undergoes extra lateral friction. The lighter the tone arm and the more easily it can swivel, the less will be the lateral friction.

The last point is of particular importance when playing stereo records. As the tone arm involves horizontal friction, an increasing weight will cause greater friction on the outer sidewalls of the groove. This is heard in the form of distortion of the L channel [19]. There is a definite relationship between contact pressure, weight compensation, tone arm bearing and radius of the tone arm. The quality of playback equipment can be properly assessed only if all these points are taken into account. It would be very ridiculous, for instance, to use a 25 μm stylus with a load of 8 p where a 12 μm stylus with a load of 1 p is prescribed.

Record players are tested with special records so that the reproduction quality can be very accurately assessed. A proposal, which has so far not yet been adopted [45] is to make gramophone records with square-wave signals to assess both stereo and mono record players. Such a test record would have to contain in-phase square-wave signals for all usual speeds as well as two equal square-wave signals with a phase shift of 180° between them — for the usual speeds $33^1/_3$ and 45 rev./min. By means of such test records much time could be saved.

6.2 Tape recorders

The record head, playback head and wiper head of a tape recorder can be roughly compared to the pick-up head of a record player. A tape speed of 9.5 cm/sec implies that after 100 operating hours over 34 km of sound tape has travelled along these heads. It will be clear, therefore, that no matter how smooth the surface of the sound tape used, and how finely polished the heads may be, there is always some wear, and dust begins to collect. Nowadays cleaning tapes can be obtained by means of which the heads can be cleaned in a few minutes. But that is not the main thing to be borne in mind when testing tape recorders.

Tape recorders are tested both qualitatively and quantitatively with what are known as reference tapes [46]. These are available for tape speeds of 76, 38, 19 and 9.5 cm/sec. Initially they were made only for the usual studio speeds of 76 and 38 cm/sec. Technicians should at any rate have such test tapes for the speeds of 19 and 9.5 cm/sec. In many cases they are even used by serious tape amateurs. Such a reference tape consists of four sections for level tone, gap adjustment, frequency response and no load respectively. All recordings occupy the whole width of the reference tape, i.e. they are full track recordings. A spoken introduction is given at the beginning and between adjacent sections. A tube voltmeter and an oscilloscope are sufficient to carry out measurements with the reference tape. Further details are given in the drawing of Fig. 6.6. The actual matter recorded on the various tapes is summarised in Table 6.1.

It should be carefully noted that there are also older types of reference tapes with different recordings on the market. In principle all measurements carried out with reference tapes — they could even have square wave signals analogous to the test records mentioned in Section 6.1 — include the playback head of the relevant tape recorder, for after all the whole reproduction

TABLE 6.1

Recording	95 cm/sec	19 cm/sec	38 and 76 cm/sec
Level tone for gap adjustment	333 ± 1 c/s 10 kc/s	1,000 ± 3 c/s 10 kc/s	1,000 ± 3 c/s 10 kc/s
Frequency response	333 c/s	1 kc/s	1 kc/s
	333 c/s	1 kc/s	1 kc/s
	31.5 c/s	31.5 c/s	31.5 c/s
	40 c/s	10 c/s	40 c/s
	63 c/s	63 c/s	63 c/s
	125 c/s	125 c/s	125 c/s
	250 c/s	250 c/s	250 c/s
	500 c/s	500 c/s	500 c/s
	1 kc/s	1 kc/s	1 kc/s
	2 kc/s	2 kc/s	2 kc/s
	4 kc/s	4 kc/s	4 kc/s
	6.3 kc/s	6.3 kc/s	6.3 kc/s
	8 kc/s	8 kc/s	8 kc/s
	10 kc/s	10 kc/s	10 kc/s
	12.5 kc/s	12.5 kc/s	12.5 kc/s
	333 c/s	16 kc/s	16 kc/s
		1 kc/s	18 kc/s
			1 kc/s

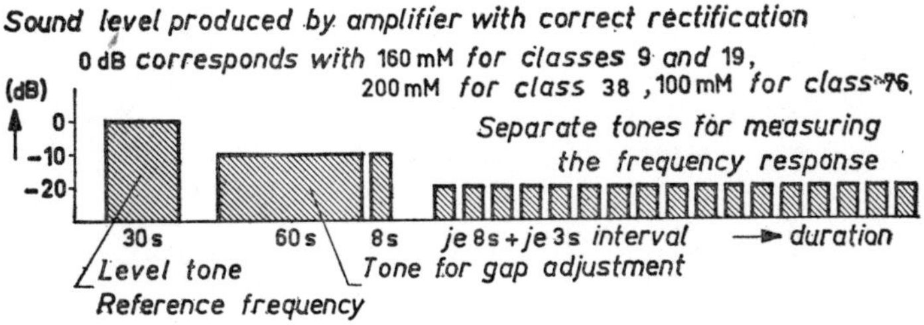

Fig. 6.6. Diagram of recordings on reference tapes

chain with all its components must be tested. In Section 6.3 testing the amplifier in a tape recorder will be discussed in detail as otherwise so many points would have to be explained twice.

6.3 The amplifier

Nowadays testing amplifiers by means of square-wave signals is being adopted on a continuously expanding scale, due to the many advantages offered [45, 47, 48]. A great deal of time can be saved in testing the frequency response as well as the stability of amplifiers. Several measurements are carried out simultaneously. The relationships resemble those obtained when using a wobbulator for testing HF amplifiers. In a similar way the transmission characteristics of active as well as passive four-poles can be ascertained by means of square wave signals.

For the correct interpretation of the test results it is very important to know the maximum permissible distortion of a square-wave signal led through a test sample. Particularly in the LF range a square-wave signal should not be distorted at all, as the bandwidth of the LF amplifier is already narrow. Therefore the distortion phenomena and their origin should be known [45].

In short, we may say that mathematical analysis of a square-wave signal shows that the latter consists of a sinusoidal voltage with a basic frequency f_1 and a number of sinusoidal components having frequencies of $3f_1$, $5f_1$, $7f_1$, etc. The amplitudes of these uneven harmonics are inversely proportional to the frequency, see Fig. 6.7 [48].

As already mentioned in the foregoing, square-wave signals fed into LF amplifiers are always distorted, for which there may be different causes. Fig. 6.8 shows a few characteristic distortions which will be explained in the following [48]. If a square-wave signal shows no distortion at the output (see Section 6.8a), it is almost certain that sinusoidal signals with frequencies of ten or twenty times that of the square-wave signal will hardly show any amplitude or phase distortion either.

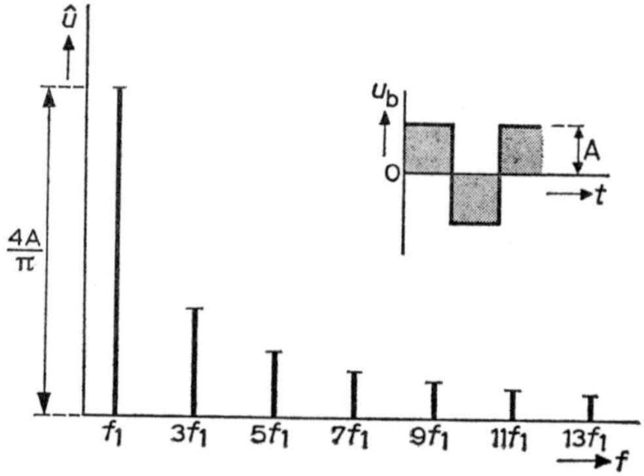

Fig. 6.7. Analysis of a symmetrical square-wave signal; the uneven harmonics are inversely proportional to the frequency

If the square-wave signal shows horizontal distortion, that is to say if the horizontal part of the pulse slants, while the flanks remain perpendicular, this points to distorted LF frequency transmission. A curve form shown in Fig. 6.8b indicates amplitude damping and a phase error in the basic wave of the adjusted square-wave signal and the lower harmonics. Distortion corresponding to Fig. 6.8c is a worse case of that described in Fig. 6.8b. The slanting top is caused mainly by the coupling and de-coupling capacitors used in the amplifier.

If however, the flanks of the square-wave signals show distortion while the tops remain horizontal, there is a high-frequency fault somewhere. For instance, if a curve according to Fig. 6.8d appears at the output of the amplifier under test, this points to reduced amplification of the higher harmonics of the selected square-wave signal, while there is also a phase error

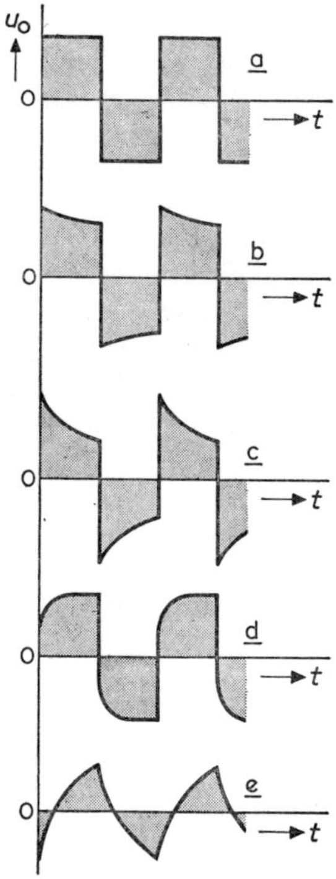

Fig. 6.8. Various kinds of distortion of the symmetrical square wave signal as found when testing amplifiers. Each figure is explained in the text

between the various components. If the output signal looks like Fig. 6.8e, these phenomena are even more pronounced. Distortion of the flanks is mainly caused by the input and output capacitances of the electron tubes or transistors, and the parasitic (wiring) capacitance.

If the graphs of Fig. 6.8 refer to an amplifier, the frequency response of the latter would look like Fig. 6.9 [48]. If this *RC*-coupled amplifier were to receive square-wave signals of the frequencies indicated by the arrows above the curve, the output signals would have forms corresponding with the graphs of Fig. 6.8 indicated with the same letters. This is a quick way of obtaining an overall impression of the amplitude and phase distortion of an amplifier.

In practice the following procedure is followed to determine the lowest frequency response of an amplifier with sufficient accuracy, using a square-wave generator, e.g. type GM 2314 or GM 2324 [45]. The frequency of the square-wave signal is varied until the starting points of all pulses form a straight line, then the generator setting is read off. This method can be used for non-compensated LF amplifiers. For amplifiers with compensated frequency response it is recommended first to adjust the bass and treble controls to normal position. If the lower frequency response is too low, all *CR* and *RC* circuits should be checked, for instance:

— Grid capacitors
— Cathode capacitors
— Grid leak resistors and coupling capacitors
— Shifted operating point of a tube — caused by a defective leak resistor or a vacuum fault in the tube — can be the cause of poor bass frequencies.
— A high-ohmic (!) short circuit in the output transformer can cause the same faults

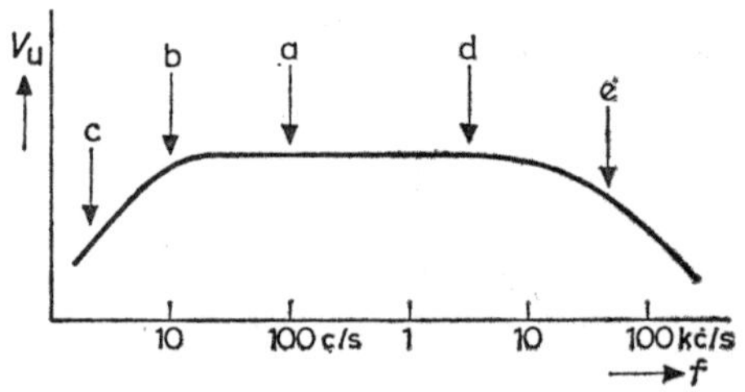

Fig. 6.9. Frequency response of an amplifier with indication of the square-wave distortions shown in Fig. 6.8

— Frequency-setting components in feedback networks also have a certain effect on the lower frequency response.

If all the effects of a reproduction circuit must be determined, the signal should, for instance, be fed to the amplifier input while the voltage drop across a low-resistance of about 0.5—1 Ω connected in series with the speech coil of the loudspeaker is displayed on an oscilloscope. In this way the current through the speech coil is checked. We know that loudspeaker current and voltage are not in phase throughout the reproduction range. In electrodynamic loudspeakers, however, the converted energy is proportional to the current. To avoid extra distortion caused by the oscilloscope, it is recommended to use an oscilloscope with a d.c. amplifier for the bottom of the LF band.

To measure the highest frequency response of an amplifier with a square-wave generator the following procedure can be adopted [45]. A square-wave signal with a repetition frequency of about 2 — 3 kc/s is applied to the amplifier input. At a maximum frequency response of 10 — 15 kc/s the frequency ratio will then be about 1/5 (approximate value). At such a ratio the square-wave signal is not yet integrated. The voltage height displayed on the screen of the oscilloscope is observed for each peak and if necessary adjusted to a certain value by controlling the *y*-amplifier in the oscilloscope. The frequency of the square-wave signal (this signal must be absolutely symmetrical) is then increased until the image on the screen (peak-to-peak) has been reduced to 51.8 % or practically half the original setting. Of course the output voltage of the square-wave generator should not vary with the frequency, which is indeed not the case with generators GM 2314 and GM 2324. If an amplifier output does not reach the indicated values, there is a deficiency in high frequency response. Then the following components must be checked:

— The external resistors of pentode amplifier stages as regards resistance increase
— HF filter resistance in the LF channel of the demodulator as regards resistance increase
— *RC* circuits in the feedback network
— Amplifier triodes as regards internal resistance
— Output transformers as regards leakage
— Amplifier output as regards mismatch, e.g. overmatching of loudspeaker

All investigations can, of course, be carried out step by step. This is especially recommended if a fault is to be located in a reproduction circuit.

There are two possible methods. Either a suitable square-wave signal is applied to the input of the amplifier stage after the stage is scanned with the oscilloscope, or the oscilloscope is connected to the amplifier output while the signal is fed into each successive amplifier stage.

A square-wave generator is also indispensable when testing the stability of compensated LF amplifiers with LF transformers, for instance [45]. The sudden power transient of the square-wave signal more or less excites any damped oscillator circuit contained in the equipment under test, thus producing damped oscillations. This method is known as 'overshoot'. If the amplifier were tested with sinusoidal oscillations, no such overshoot would occur. The amplifier would then most probably be classified as good. But if piano music, for instance, is transmitted it would immediately become obvious that the sound reproduction is by no means satisfactory. Trying to find the fault with sinusoidal oscillations or a distortion meter would be a mere waste of time. It would be far more useful to check the pulse ratio. Particularly in amplifiers fitted with LF transformers or several feedback networks as well as in output stages with positive feedback, slight instabilities are liable to occur, and especially if the value of the damping resistance has changed. Sometimes amplifiers have different feedback channels for different frequencies. If the transmission characteristic of such a feedback channel varies, this may result in a positive feedback of its own or neighbouring frequencies. In all these cases square-wave signals can be used for testing.

For stereo reproduction two amplifiers are needed. Each of them must amplify their input frequencies without any amplitude or phase distortion [45]. The corresponding controls of the two amplifiers are interconnected so that the transmission characteristics of both channels can be varied simultaneously. Moreover, there is the balancing network, the stereo balance adjusting the gain of the two channels to exactly the same value. Here too, square-wave signals can be used for testing purposes. The simplest method is to connect the generator to the amplifier inputs alternately. For occasional testing this system is usually satisfactory, whereas for regular testing special accessories must be used. Fig. 6.10 shows two circuits with test leads. With the input lead the square-wave signal can be simultaneously applied to both the amplifier inputs. The input adapter is merely a socket connected to the generator, and fitted with a five-pin plug at the output end. The centre contact of the socket is connected to the corresponding plug pin via two equal resistors of a value ranging from 10 — 100 kΩ. The resistance value depends on the required decoupling factor. In most cases the amplifier outputs

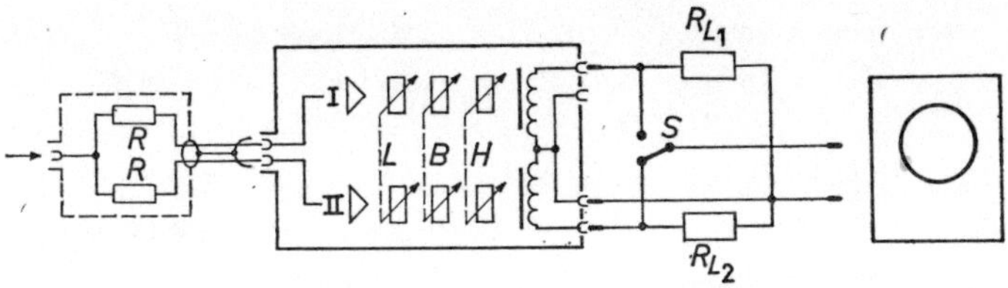

Fig. 6.10. Two circuit with leads for testing amplifiers

are so designed that any built-in loudspeakers are automatically switched off. This arrangement can be used to make an output adapter which, apart from the two plugs, contains a single-pole switch *S* and two resistors. The resistors have the same value and serve to replace the terminating impedance of the built-in loudspeaker. With switch *S* the output signal of the two channels can be applied to the input of the oscilloscope. By operating the switch, the output signals of the two channels can now easily be compared with each other.

Of course, the testing methods employed for amplifiers can readily be used for tape recorders too. There are still other applications for square-wave signals [45]. The bandwidth of a reproduction channel, and particularly the maximum frequency requirement, is in fact more important in tape recorders. As the characteristics of magnetic recording are not linear with the frequency special measures must be taken in their design to make them suitable for recording and playback purposes. Owing to these measures the amplifier channels show a pronounced tendency towards overshoot when tested with square-wave signals. As the upper frequency limit is different for each tape speed, the apparatus must, of course, be tested with the speed selector switch in all positions while the correcting networks are also changed over.

The frequency response of the recording amplifier of a channel, for instance, can easily be tested for one or more tape speeds and afterwards compared with the other channels. For that purpose a square-wave signal of say 1 kc/s, is applied to the input and the oscillogram of the recording current or voltage observed. The recording current can be displayed on the oscilloscope by leading it through a small resistor, about 100 Ω, which is included in the 'cold' conductor of the recording or combined head. A number of tape recorders are already fitted with such measuring resistor. With equipment fitted with a low-ohmic recording head the much higher voltage can be picked up immediately at the head. This applies especially to transistor tape recorders. The oscillogram clearly showing overshoot tells us how bad the distortion is. The resonance frequency can be found by comparing the cycle times.

Playback distortion can best be measured with a test tape carrying suitable high square-wave frequency signals. Such tape is a valuable member in the range of existing test tapes. However, so long as these tapes are not obtainable in the market, those interested will have to make their own.

6.4 Loudspeakers

As already said before (see Section 2.3), technicians usually have to accept loudspeakers for what they are. Damaged cones and soiled air gaps are immediately spotted.

Soiled air gaps in electro-dynamic speakers can easily be cleaned [49]. All that is needed is a thin 5 mm wide strip of good quality transformer sheet iron. This strip is run through the air gap. Any metal particles the gap may hold — and these are the most important — adhere to the metal strip and can thus be easily removed. They can be wiped off the strip at a suitable distance. After having inserted the strip into the gap few times, even the smallest particle of iron will have been removed. Any other dust particles left behind can be easily removed by blowing. The principle of the procedure is that the strip of metal used for transformer cores and dynamo armatures has a high permeability so that it attracts all metal particles which have been magnetised in the air gap.

Another point deserving attention in stereo installations is that the loudspeakers should be connected the right way round.

It is important for the loudspeakers to oscillate in phase with each other. A great deal of disappointment can be avoided by taking the trouble to test the polarity of the loudspeakers used in one sound installation by means of a d.c. source, a flash-light battery, for instance. When this low d.c. voltage is applied, the cones of the loudspeaker make one movement in a particular direction and stay there till the voltage is removed. All that need be done now is to see whether the cones assume the same position, either 'out' or 'in'. The terminals can be suitably marked with a modern felt pen.

CHAPTER 7

TESTING HF STEREOPHONY DECODERS

As was the case for Chapter 6, dealing with the testing of LF stereo playback equipment, in the present chapter, dealing with the testing of HF stereophony decoders, a full description does not lie within the scope of this book.

For all work carried out on HF and LF stereo equipment it is possible to some extent to separate the HF and LF parts. It is far more difficult, however, to make this separation between the parts in a radio transmitter serving for both mono and stereo transmission, than in equipment used for stereo transmission only. In the first place it is impossible to 'lift out' the decoder as a separate unit! Even if this were possible, the performance of the decoder alone is not the only factor in the performance of the complete apparatus. This implies that the input signal to the decoder is also important for the quality of stereo reception.

This starts at the aerial. When the 'Südwestfunk' broadcast its first stereo music (see Table 3.1), many letters were received from listeners [50]. Although these were unanimous in expressing their gratitude, a surprisingly large percentage of them complained about loud noise interference during stereo reception, which was not heard in mono reception. Measurements carried out in the laboratories of this broadcasting company showed that with a few exceptions the receivers needed a useful signal ranging from 100 to 300 μV across 240 Ω for stereo reception. This in contrast with mono reception where a few millivolts are sufficient. This becomes clear when surveying the particular topography of the transmitter service area (see Fig. 3.1). In the more favourable level areas high field intensities are easily obtained. It should be noted, however, that stereo transmission always involves a loss inherent in the system, amounting to about 30 dB.

Naturally this is taken into account when designing a radio receiver. It is equally certain that no matter the quality of the receiver components, they cannot produce what the aerial fails to give. HF stereo fans as well as technicians will have to get used to the idea that the built-in auxiliary dipole has no function in stereo reception. It is an entirely wrong policy to buy an expensive stereo receiver with the idea that 'if it is expensive it is good', and then to try and save money on the aerial. One might just as well conceive the idea of saving on the electric installation at the expense of a 10—20% voltage drop. As regards the aerial we also have to consider *cause* and *effect*. One must not jump to the conclusion that the values mentioned in the foregoing will be improved in the near future.

As in all radio servicing, stereo decoders too, must be tested methodically. The signal must be traced through the apparatus, and any deviations from set values measured. This, of course, includes the measuring of nominal voltages. But all this is not enough to provide a complete test on a decoder. A definite answer is only found after a final test with a complete stereo signal has been made. Similarly the degree of cross-talk compensation (see Sections 5.1, 5.2 and 5.3) can only be adjusted under the same conditions, and only in the apparatus of which the decoder forms part. This is because the characteristics of the IF amplifier are involved in this particular adjustment.

It should be understood that a stereo signal generator is used to supply the complete stereo signal (see Section 8.4). If, as often happens, such a generator is not at the moment available, the test signals transmitted from the various radio stations can be used instead [51]. Each station has its individual signal code and pattern and it is a wise precaution to obtain details from the stations concerned, to facilitate servicing at a customer's home even though a stereo signal generator is available. Table 7.1, for instance, gives the stereo test signals transmitted by the Norddeutschen and Westdeutschen Rundfunk respectively. Signal 1 serves for tuning the various oscillating circuits of the decoder. The remaining signals can be used the same way as signals from a stereo generator.

Furthermore, extra test signals are transmitted via metronomes operating at different rhythms to check the polarity of loudspeakers (not to be confused with the polarity check of the loudspeaker terminals described in Section 6.4).

Finally a few notes on the signal sequence and the adjustment of the switch decoder [40] discussed in Section 5.1. Satisfactory operation of the decoder depends on the correct functioning of the switch diodes as well as on the cross-talk compensation. A first condition is a sharp separation between the pilot tone and its amplification and doubling in the correct amplitude and phase. The next step after checking the d.c. operating point is to trace the path of the pilot tone by means of an oscilloscope. A certain criterion can already be observed in the stereo indicator (see Section 5.4).

TABLE 7.1

No.	Signal, level L	R	Duration (min.)	Application
1	Announcement via both channels followed by two counter-phase 1 kc/s signals, one in the *L* and one in the *R* channel (difference signal), modulation depth abt. 38 kc/s.		2	Tuning the oscillating circuit for pilot tone, subcarrier and transmitted difference signal
2	Announcement followed by a 1 kc/s signal, modulation depth abt. 38 kc/s	no signal	1	Compensating LF cross talk in the *R* channel
3	no signal	announcement followed by a 1 kc/s signal, modulation depth abt. 38 kc/s	1	Compensating LF cross talk in the *L* channel
4	Announcement followed by a 5 kc/s signal, modulation depth abt. 38 kc/s	no signal	1	Compensating HF cross talk in the *R* channel
5	no signal	announcement followed by a 5 kc/s signal, modulation depth abt. 38 kc/s	1	Compensating HF cross talk in the *L* channel

Depending on the amplitude of the signal from the stereo signal generator a voltage of a certain amplitude will occur between the input of transistor TS201 and the output of transistor TS202 (see Section 5.4). The nominal value can best be found by comparison with a reference decoder (if available), or it can be judged from experience. All resonant circuits are next tuned to maximum level. Before being applied to the input of transistor TS201, the 19 kc/s pilot tone is given a phase lead of about 45° by means of capacitor C202.

The necessity for this phase shift is illustrated by Fig. 7.1. Fig. 7.1a shows the transmitted 19 kc/s pilot tone for a 38 kc/s switching signal or suppressed sub-carrier. Simultaneously with a zero crossing of the pilot tone, the 38 kc/s signal crosses zero from negative to positive. Fig. 7.1b shows how the 19 kc/s pilot tone is doubled to 38 kc/s by means of full-wave rectification. One component of the resulting pulse signal is an alternating voltage whose zero axis is indicated by the broken line. This alternating voltage of twice the frequency of the pilot tone is not sinusoidal. But the purely sinusoidal component can, however, be filtered out. As Fig. 7.1c shows, the negative and

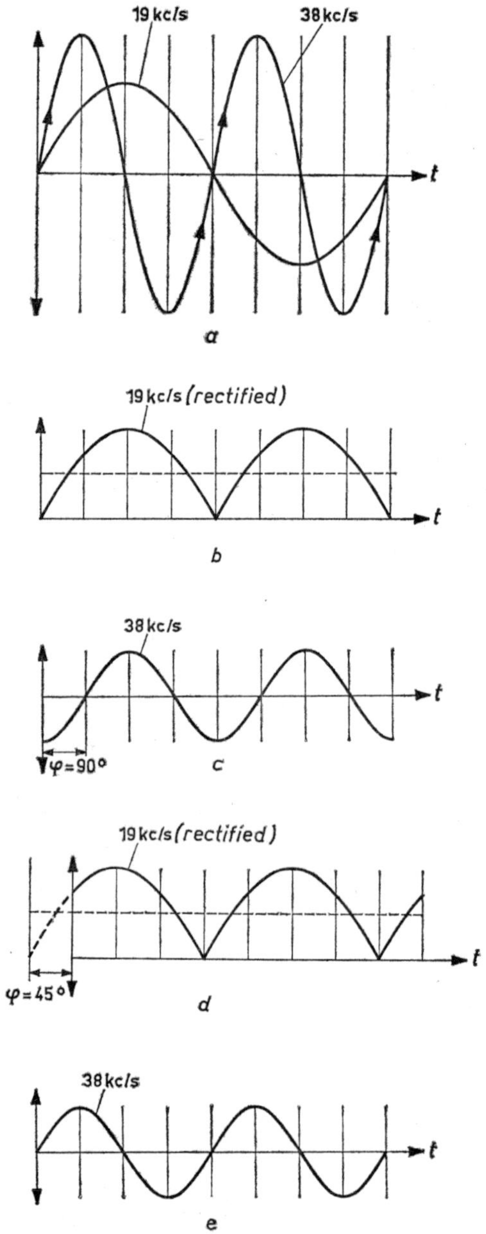

Fig. 7.1. The switching decoder requires a 45° phase lead of the pilot tone. Each diagram is described separately in the text

positive maximum values of the filtered-out sinusoidal 38 kc/s voltage correspond to the maximum values of the non-sinusoidal voltage. Consequently the resulting 38 kc/s voltage (see Fig. 7.1a) has a phase lag of 90°. The phase shift can easily be compensated with the pilot tone. The 45° phase shift required for that purpose is obtained by means of the *RC* circuit formed by capacitor C202 and the active input impedance of the stage containing transistor TS201. Fig. 7.1d shows the graph of the pilot tone with a lead of 45° after rectification. With respect to the 38 kc/s signal the phase shift is exactly 90°. Fig. 7.1e illustrates the resemblance between the 38 kc/s signal after filtering out the basic sine wave, and the required phase relationship shown in Fig. 7.1a.

This explains why capacitor C202 has such an important function. Any variation in capacitance at the input impedance of transistor TS201 finds its expression in a phase shift. The decoder can then no longer switch over at the right instant, and this in turn is reflected in an increase of cross-talk. It is therefore advisable to test the decoder after the apparatus has warmed up sufficiently (about 15 min.). On the other hand the apparatus housing the decoder is excessively heated by an additional flow of air as produced by the output stage, for instance.

Once systematic tracing of the 19 kc/s (38 kc/s) signal proves that if the amplitude values are correct, cross-talk can be minimised by adjusting the phase. In doing so, cross-talk compensation is first cancelled out by adjusting resistor R213 to its minimum value. Coil S106 of the stereo generator adjusted to *L* or *R*, is then shifted until cross-talk is at minimum. Finally, the residual voltages inherent in the system are brought to optimum value by adjusting resistor R213. This optimum value is found after several change-overs between *L* and *R* and a repeated re-setting of resistor R213. This is due to certain asymmetries so that there can be only an optimum but no minimum adjustment.

Should the LF signal still contain a strong 38 kc/s component, or should amplitude differences occur between the two channels, this may be due to defective or badly-matched switch diodes.

CHAPTER 8

MEASURING AND TESTING INSTRUMENTS

In considering the measuring and testing instruments required, the scope of this chapter is limited to giving general directions and recommendations. The range of instruments obtainable is enormous [52], while at the same time the cost involved usually depends on the measurements and tests to be carried out. We will content ourselves, therefore in this chapter by describing a number of instruments with outstanding possibilities for the technical man.

8.1 Universal measuring instruments

It may perhaps be a waste of words to say anything at all about the universal measuring instrument. But there is a reason for doing so. Such an instrument is of course a very handy one. It is *the* instrument for easy transportation although it should not just be stuffed away in a corner of the tool kit. A first requirement is that while measurements are being made the load on the system under investigation should be kept at a minimum. There are of course a number of measurements where the load presented by the measuring instrument is irrelevant. This should not always be assumed to be the case, however, and due consideration must be given to avoid sensitive apparatus, not designed for heavy loads, being measured with instruments which have a relatively low internal impedance, thus giving readings which are very misleading. Another factor not be to underestimated is the accuracy of the instrument, or rather, the 'measuring error'.

Fig. 8.1 gives the front view of a universal instrument P 817 00/02 suitable for servicing purposes. It contains a resiliently suspended meter having no less than 28 ranges, and thus providing ample choice of the most favourable scale range for any given test. For d.c. and a.c. voltages and currents the measuring error is about 3% f.s.d. The dial carries five scales: three for current and voltage measurements, one for resistance measurements and one for measuring voltage levels from —10 . . . +12 dB. The latter type of

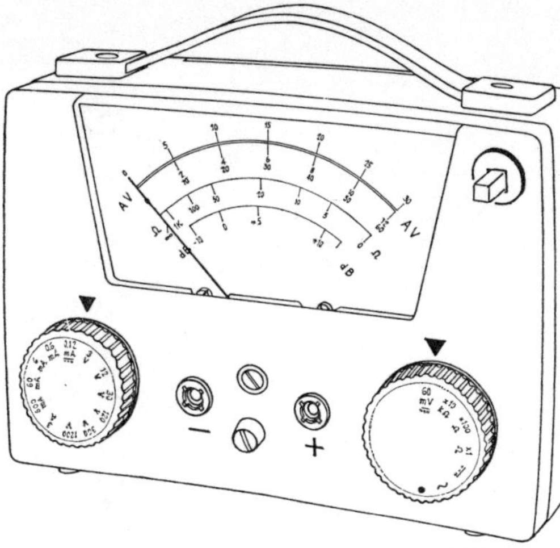

PEM 1403

Fig. 8.1. Universal measuring instrument P 817 00/02

measurements are based on a scale in which 0 dB = 0.775 V across 600 Ω (1 mW).

The meter is protected against momentary overloads by two diodes except for the 30 μA d.c. and 60 mV d.c. ranges as for these values the system under test is connected direct to the sockets of the instrument. For d.c. voltage measurements the internal resistance is 40 kΩ/V except for the 60 mV range, for which it is 3.33 kΩ/V. The corresponding value for a.c. voltage measurements is 1,666 Ω/V for a frequency range from 30 to 10,000 c/s, except for the 1,200 V range (30 — 5,000 c/s). For a.c. current measurements in the range from 30 — 300 c/s the scale can be expanded to 300 A by means of an extra current transformer.

The latest innovation in universal measuring instruments is the automatic protection against overload. The complete circuit diagram is given in Fig. 8.2.

8.2 Electronic voltmeter

In view of the wide range of measuring problems, a whole series of electronic voltmeters have been developed. Table 8.1 gives a rough but comprehensive

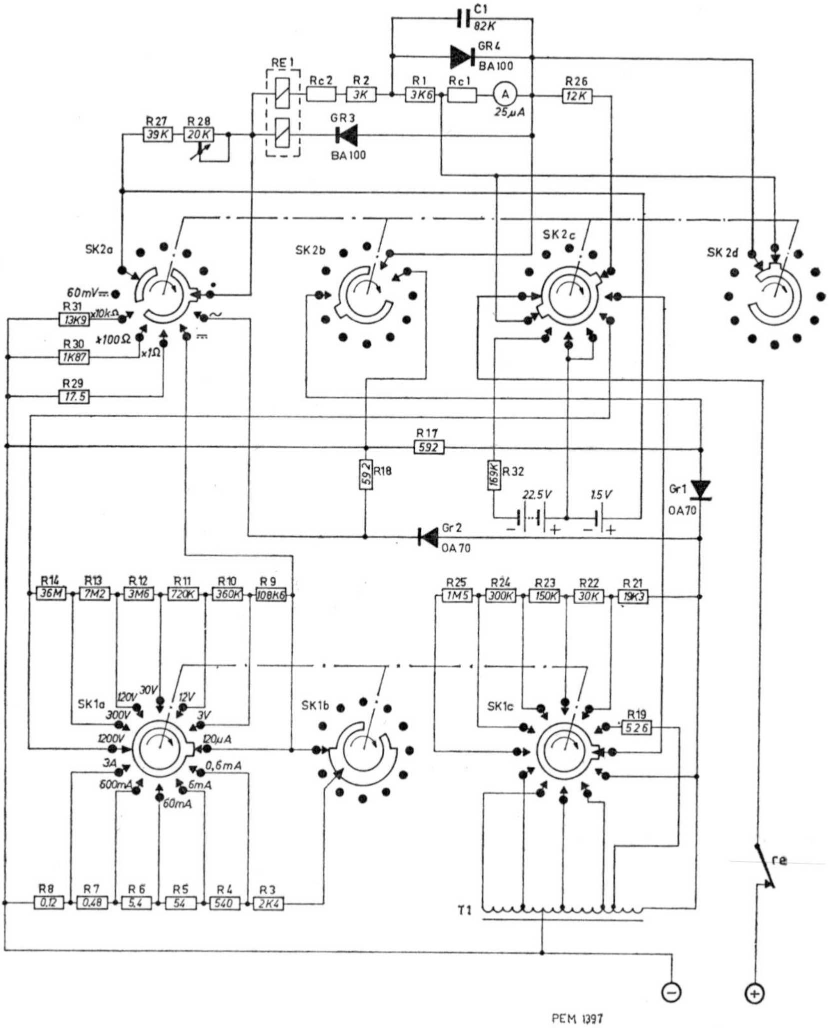

Fig. 8.2. Circuit diagram of universal measuring instrument P 817 00/02

survey of the various types [52]. A detailed account of an instrument of this series, particularly suitable for rapid measuring is given below. This is the electronic voltmeter PM 2405, an analogue electronic instrument in which the most suitable measuring range is automatically selected by a special

	Frequency range		a.c. voltage range		d.c. voltage range		Input impedance		Resistance range	
	c/s	Mc/s	mV	V	mV	V	mΩ	pF	Ω	MΩ
PM 2430					1 1000	0,03 300 *)	1 100			
GM 6020					0,1 10	10 1000	1 100	02/15 10		
GM 6023	10	1	10	300			1,5	15 . . . 25		
PM 2520	10	1	1	300			8/20	15/7.5		
GM 6012	2	1	1	300			4 10	20 10		
PM 2453	10	5	1	300			1	35 15		
PM 2451	10	7	1	30			1 10	30 10		
GM 6041	1 k	30	1	30			0,05 . . . 1 2 . . . 50	7 2		
GM 6025	100 k	1000	10	10			0,035 . . . 0,065	1		
PM 2401	10	0,1	100	300	100	300 *)	1 . . . 10 (—) 1 . . . 10 (~)	15 . . . 25	1	10
GM 6000	20	100	1000	300	1000	1000 *)	10 (—) 3 (~)	8	10	5
PM 2405	20	600	500	300	500	500 *)	10 (—) 1,3 (~)	3,5	10	100
GM 6001	20	1000	1000	300	300	1000 *)	10 . . . 100 (—) 0,07 . . . 3 (~)	2 3,5	10	10

*) with HT measuring probe up to 30 kV
(—) d.c.
(~) a.c.

electric motor [53]. Furthermore, in d.c. measurement the polarity is tested and indicated. Measurements in which the orders of magnitude are unknown, or which are carried out by unskilled operators, are greatly facilitated by the built-in automatic device which prevents the wrong range being used.

The instrument, the block diagram of which is shown in Fig. 8.3 is suitable for d.c. measurements between 50 mV and 500 V, a.c. measurements between 50 mV and 300 V and resistance measurements between 1 Ω and 100 MΩ. The instrument is prepared for use by merely depressing a push-button corresponding to a particular measurement. All further operations are automatically performed when the system under test is connected to the instrument. A lamp illuminating the appropriate meter scale facilitates meter reading. For d.c. measurements the automatic device also ensures the correct polarity which is also indicated by a pilot lamp.

The basic measuring circuit consists of a bridge circuit formed by two triodes and two resistors. Measuring instrument M_1 as well as the so-called switching instrument M_2 are connected between the cathodes of the two triodes. Each of the triodes is preceded by a cathode follower ensuring feed-back independent of the output impedance of the bridge diode. The measured voltage affects the bridge equilibrium, thus causing the instruments to show

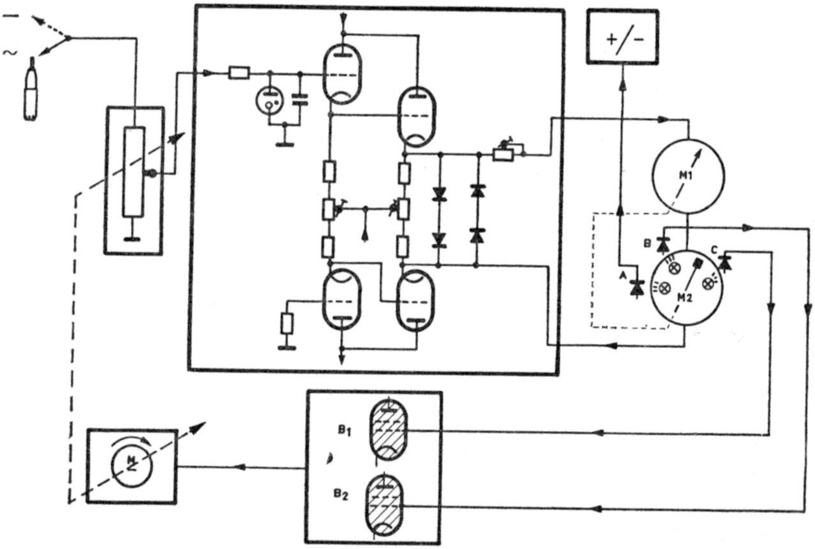

Fig. 8.3. Block diagram of automatic electronic voltmeter PM 2405

a corresponding deflection. A special rectifier probe is also supplied for a.c. measurements. Resistors are measured with a constant voltage.

Switching instrument M_2 serves for automatic selection of the measuring range. It has the same electrical values as instrument M_1, but is also fitted with three photo diodes located to the left (*A*), at one third of the scale (*B*), and the end of the scale (*C*) respectively. A small incandescent lamp is fitted directly opposite each of the diodes. The light beam from one or other of these lamps can be intercepted by a vane carried by the pointer of the instrument.

Initially the lowest measuring range is always switched on. In case the wrong polarity has been chosen or if the polarity of the input voltage is reversed, the error is corrected by light diode *A*. If, when probing the system under measurement the instrument gives full-scale deflection, the next higher measuring range is automatically switched on by light diode *C*, thyratron B_1 and electric motor *M*. This procedure is repeated until the most suitable measuring range not exceeding the maximum range has been found. If, for instance, the measured voltage drops so far that the light beam incident on light diode *B* is intercepted, the measuring range selector is started again.

This switching over takes place during d.c., a.c. and resistance measurements. The average switching time for voltage measurements is about 2 seconds, and for resistance measurements 3 seconds. In the most unfavourable case 4 and 6 seconds respectively are needed to cover all scale ranges. If a certain range must be maintained throughout the measurement, it is only necessary to change over the switch from 'AUTO' to 'HOLD'. The selected condition is also indicated by a pilot lamp. When the instrument is disconnected, the initial 'AUTO' position is automatically restored.

8.3 Oscilloscopes

More than any other measuring instrument, the oscilloscope has in the course of a few decades become an indispensable universal measuring instrument. There is ample literature dealing with special circuits in which the oscilloscope can be used [54, 55], so that as with electronic voltmeters it would lead too far to discuss this instrument in detail. It will suffice therefore, to give a brief survey. The principal data of several typical oscilloscopes are given in table 8.2 [52]. One instrument, namely the double-beam oscilloscope type PM 3230, which is largely transistorised [56], deserves special mention.

The block diagram of double-beam oscilloscope PM 3230 is given in Fig. 8.4. Thanks to the transistorised circuits, the power consumption of the apparatus is no more than 70 W, while its weight of 11 kg is relatively low. The two *Y*-amplifiers are identical. The time-base generator can be triggered via a *Y*-amplifier or externally; the polarity can be varied. For technical data consult Table 8.2.

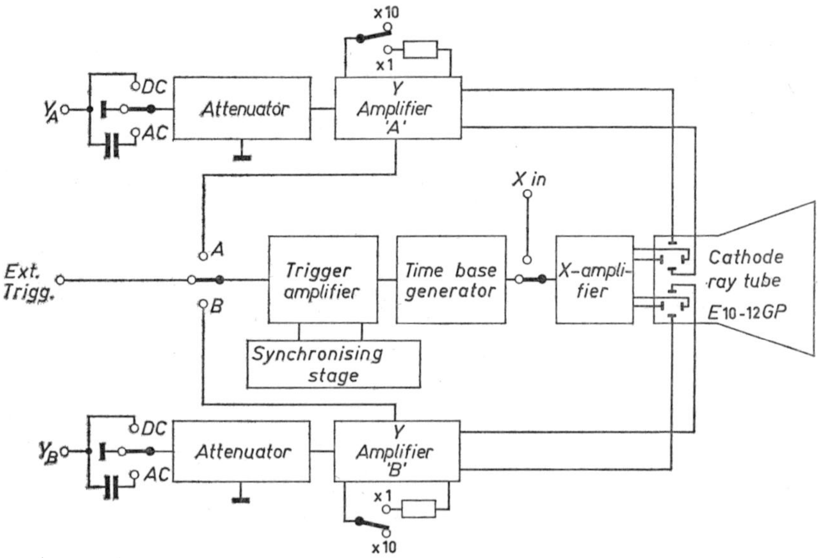

Fig. 8.4. Block diagram of double-beam oscilloscope PM 3230

8.4 Square-wave signal generator

A square-wave signal generator is especially required for testing amplifiers as described in Section 6.3. Square-wave generator GM 2314 supplies a signal which, after appropriate attenuation, is particularly suitable for testing stereo amplifier channels. This generator, the block diagram of which is shown in Fig. 8.5, is arranged for continuous frequency control in six overlapping ranges. The following outputs can be used together, the frequency and pulse width being adjusted simultaneously: (a) Square-wave pulse with

TABLE 8.2

	HF oscilloscope GM 5600 X	X-Y oscilloscope GM 5639	HF oscilloscope PM 3201	HF double-beam oscilloscope PM 3230
Cathode ray tube	DH 7-78	DN 10-78	D 10-12 GM	E 10-12 GH
Total acceleration voltage	1.6 kV	2 kV	3 kV	4 kV
Screen diameter	7 cm flat face	10 cm flat face	10 cm flat face	10 cm flat face
Graticule division	1 cm	1 cm	1 cm	0.8 cm
Y-amplifier	d.c. voltage	d.c. voltage with AC-DC switch	d.c. voltage with AC-DC switch	d.c. voltage with AC-DC switch
Frequency range *Y*	0—5 Mc/s	0—1 Mc/s	0—1 (5) Mc/s	0—1.5 (10)Mc/s
Deflection coefficients *Y*	50 mV/division	100 mV/division	10 (50) mV/division	2.5 (20) mV/division
Input voltage divider *Y*	continuous and 9 calibr. steps	continuous and 9 calibr. steps	continuous and 9 calibr. steps	continuous and 11 calibr. steps
X-amplifier	a.c.	d.c.	d.c.	d.c.
Frequency range *X*	5 c/s—2 Mc/s	0—1 Mc/s	0—300 kc/s	0—1 Mc/s
Input voltage divider *X*	continuous 3—50 V/division	continuous and 8 calibr. steps	continuous 1—50 V/division	100—500 V/division
Time base	trigg. self-oscillating	trigg. self-oscillating	trigg. self-oscillating	trigg. and autom.
Time base division	0.5 μsec division to 30 msec/division 7 calibr. steps	0.2 μsec/division to 100 msec/division 8 calibr. steps	0.5 μsec/division to 0.2 sec/division 18 calibr. steps 5× expansion	0.5 μsec/division to 0.5 sec/division 19 calibr. steps 5×expansion

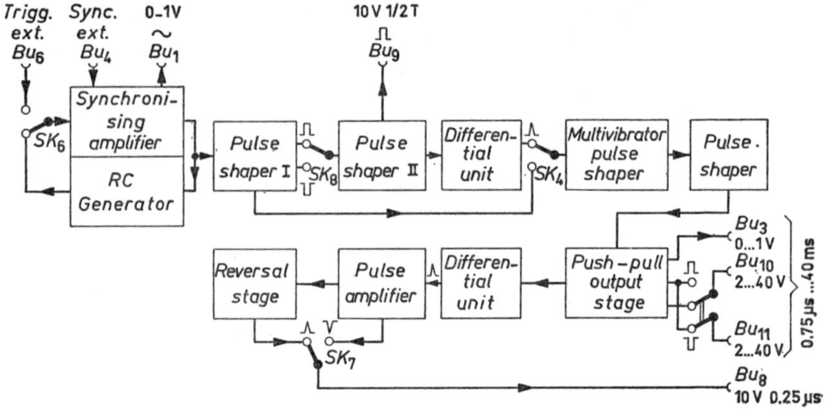

Fig. 8.5. Block diagram of a square-wave generator GM 2314

variable width, amplitude and frequency; (b) Symmetrical square-wave voltage with stable amplitude and variable frequency; (c) Narrow pulse of stable width, fixed amplitude and variable frequency. The output voltage, frequency and pulse width are immediately indicated on the scale. The rise time is 25 nsec for voltages up to 10 V_{p-p}, for higher voltages the rise time is less than 65 nsec.

Frequencies from 15 c/s . . . 200 kc/s can be adjusted in 6 ranges for all output voltages. Within each range adjustment is continuous. The scale is calibrated in cycles and periodic times.

8.5 Stereo generator

In cases where test signals transmitted by radio stations (see Chapter 7) are not sufficient, a special apparatus producing the required signals will have to be used. This apparatus is the stereo generator which is by no means merely a rough and ready servicing tool, but rather an instrument of high precision [57]. Fig. 8.6 gives the front view of such a generator; the block diagram is shown in Fig. 8.7.

The stereo generator contains two *RC* generators for 400 and 1,000 c/s respectively, which can be connected to the preamplifier. The two pre-amplifiers have a pre-emphasis of 50 μsec but can also be connected direct to the input sockets and provide a gain of 20 dB. Usually a low-pass filter follows

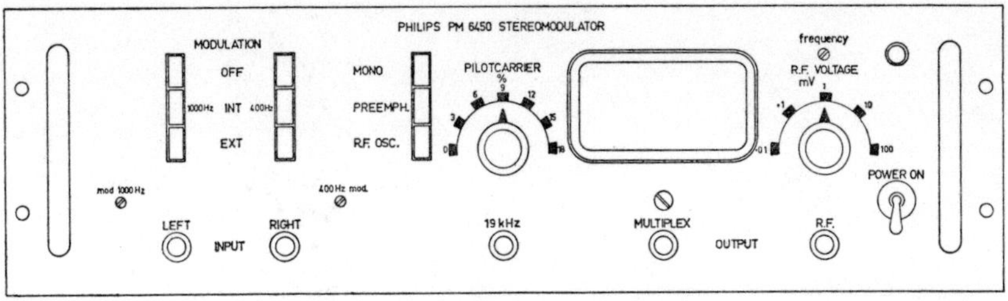

Fig. 8.6. Stereo generator PM 6450

with a blocking frequency of 19 kc/s as well as a control stage with a gain of 6 dB. The *L* and *R* signals, and also the 38 kc/s sub-carrier are fed to a ring modulator in the modulator stage to obtain the sum and difference signals. The latter is used to modulate the sub-carrier. The carrier itself is suppressed in this symmetrical modulator. The 19 kc/s carrier is produced by an oscillator which is synchronised with the 38 kc/s signal from the modulator stage.

Via a 53 kc/s low-pass filter the complete stereo signal arrives at the wide-band output amplifier which has a gain of 15 dB. The HF oscillator which is frequency-modulated with this complete stereo signal (also referred to as the multiplex signal), gives a maximum modulation depth of about 75 kc/s. The output voltage of the FM generator can be continuously adjusted by means of a logarithmic attenuator having a constant output impedance of 75 Ω. With the mode selector switch in position 'MONO' the '*L*' and '*R*' channels are connected in parallel while the pilot tone is switched off so that only the sum signal reaches the output stage and the FM unit.

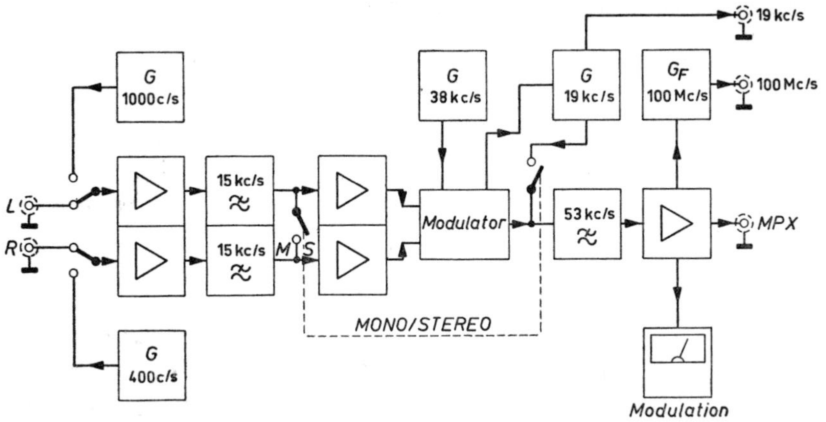

Fig. 8.7. Block diagram of stereo generator PM 6450

BIBLIOGRAPHY

[1] N. V. FRANSSEN, *Stereophony;* Philips Technical Library, Eindhoven 1964

[2] W. BÜRCK, *Physiologische Akustik;* Funkschau, Vol. **36** (1964), No. 20, p. 529-530

[3] G. J. BLEEKSMA and J. J. SCHURINK, *A loudspeaker installation for high fidelity reproduction in the home;* Philips Technical Review, Vol. **18** (1956/57), No. 10, p. 304-315

[4] DIN 45 500

[5] N. N., *Senderstereophonie – neue Technik – vollendeter Klang;* Deutsche Philips GmbH, Hamburg ,1964.

[6] N. N., *Ein Wegweiser für Tonbandfreunde;* Deutsche Philips GmbH, Hamburg, 1963

[7] *Handbuch für Hochfrequenz- und Elektro-Techniker*, Vol. I; Verlag für Radio-Foto-Kinotechnik GmbH, Berlin, 1949

[8] D. KLEIS, *Modern acoustical engineering, I: General principles;* Philips Technical Review, Vol. **20** (1958/59), No. 11, p. 309-326

[9] *Telefunken Laborbuch, Vol. 1*, 6th edition; Franzis-Verlag, München, 1964

[10] R. VERMEULEN, *A comparison between reproduced and 'live' music;* Philips Technical Review, Vol. **17** (1955/56), No. 6, p. 171-177

[11] *Handbuch für Hochfrequenz- und Elektro-Techniker, Vol. IV;* Verlag für Radio Foto Kinotechnik GmbH, Berlin, 1957

[12] R. VERMEULEN, *Stereo reverberation;* Philips Technical Review, Vol. **17** (1955/56), No. 9, p. 258-266

[13] G. BÜSCHER, *Philips Lehrbriefe, Vol. II*, 3rd edition, Deutsche Philips GmbH, Hamburg, 1962

[14] F. LANGFORD-SMITH, *Radio Designer's Handbook*, 4th edition; Iliffe & Sons, Ltd., London, 1953

[15] E. RODENHUIS, *Hi-Fi amplifier circuits;* Philips Technical Library, Eindhoven 1965

[16] N. N., *Vorschläge zur HF-Stereofonie* (Leserbrief); Funkschau, Vol. **36** (1964), No. 21, p. 1548

[17] D. H. OTTO, *Mit Luftpost aus den USA, Sonst noch was Neues;* Radio Mentor, Vol. **31** (1965), 2, p. 98

[18] DIN 45 594
[19] U. SCHMIDT, *Die Vorgänge bei der Abtastung von Schallplatten;* Funk-Technik, Vol. **19** (1964), No. 23, p. 848-850 and No. 24, p. 887-890
[20] H. G. LICHTHORN, *Schallplattentechnik – gestern und heute;* Kontakte, No. 1 (January 1965), p. 46-52; Deutsche Philips GmbH, Hamburg
[21] DIN 45 533, 45 536, 45 537, 45 546, 45 547
[22] D. A. SNEL, *Magnetic sound recording;* 3rd edition, Philips Technical Library, Eindhoven 1963
[23] DIN 45 512
[24] C. G. NIJSEN, *The tape recorder;* 2nd enlarged edition, Philips Technical Library, Eindhoven 1967
[25] H. WILLERS, *Philips* 2030 – *ein neuer High-Fidelity-Plattenspieler;* Kontakte, No. 1 (January 1965), p. 33-37; Deutsche Philips GmbH, Hamburg
[26] N. N., PHILIPS *Tonbandgeräte;* Deutsche Philips GmbH, Hamburg, 1964
[27] G. SLOT, *Audio Quality;* Philips Technical Library, Eindhoven 1964
[28] N. N., *Stereo-Verstärker* AG 9016; Deutsche Philips GmbH, Service Abteilung, Hamburg, 1963
[29] J. RODRIGUES DE MIRANDA, *Audio amplifiers with single-ended push-pull output;* Philips Technical Review, Vol. **19** (1957/58), No. 2, p. 41-49
[30] N. N., *Übertragerlose Transistor-NF-Verstärker mit Gegentakt-B-Endstufe für* 10 W *und* 2,5 W; Technische Informationen für die Industrie Nr. 49 (August 1963); Valvo GmbH, Hamburg
[31] N. N., *Ein Stereo-Heimempfänger mit Transistoren;* Technische Informationen für die Industrie Nr. 72 (December 1964); Valvo GmbH, Hamburg
[32] O. DICIOL, *„Hi-Fi“ wird genormt;* Funkschau, Vol. **37** (1965), No. 7, p. 163-165
[33] W. SCHMACKS, *Lautsprecher-Verzerrungen und Lautsprecher-Einbau;* Radio Mentor, Vol. **24** (1958), No. 6, p. 387-389
[34] B. F. LOMOW, *Ingenieurpsychologie;* Deutscher Verlag der Wissenschaften, Berlin, 1964
[35] N. N., *Stereo-Rundfunk in den Niederlanden;* Funk-Technik, Vol. **19** (1964), No. 24, p. 890
[36] N. N., *Impulse;* Funkschau, Vol. **36** (1964), No. 24, p. 641
[37] N. N., *UKW-Sendertabelle;* Deutsche Philips GmbH, Hamburg, September 1962
[38] N. N., *Sender für Rundfunk-Stereophonie;* Funk-Technik, Vol. **20** (1965), No. 5, p. 166

[39] G. Janus, *Die amerikanische FCC-Stereo-Norm;* Funk-Technik, Vol. **16** (1961), No. 16, p. 554-555
[40] N. N., *Fernlehrgang HF-Stereo-Technik;* Deutsche Philips GmbH, Service Abteilung, Hamburg
[41] H. E. Kaden, *Grundsätzliches über die HF-Stereo-Technik;* messen . . . reparieren (1964), p. 3-6; Deutsche Philips GmbH, Meßgeräte-Abteilung, Hamburg-Fuhlsbüttel
[42] N. N., *Zwei einfache Decoder für Stereo-Rundfunkempfänger;* Technische Informationen für die Industrie Nr. 52 (August 1963); Valvo GmbH, Hamburg
[43] N. N., AM/FM-*Wechselstrom-Super Capella Reverbeo* B 7 X 43 A; Deutsche Philips GmbH, Service-Abteilung, Hamburg, 1963
[44] N. N., AM/FM-*Wechselstrom-Super Capella Stereo-Truhe* F 8 D 41 A; Deutsche Philips GmbH, Service-Abteilung, Hamburg, 1964
[45] W. Schultz, *Measuring and testing with square wave signals*, Philips Technical Library, Eindhoven 1966
[46] DIN 45 513
[47] N. N., *Verstärkerprüfung mit Rechteckschwingungen;* Funktechnische Arbeitsblätter Mv 71, 2nd edition (April 1965); Franzis-Verlag, München
[48] A. C. J. Beerens, *Measuring methods and devices in electronics*, Philips Technical Library, Eindhoven 1966
[49] G. W. Schanz, *Reinigung des Luftspaltes dynamischer Lautsprecher leicht gemacht;* Radio-Magazin, Vol. **29** (1953), No. 1, p. 29
[50] K. Tetzner, *Stereofonie in der Entwicklung;* Funkschau, Vol. **37** (1965), No. 7, p. 161
[51] F. Gutschmidt, *Service-Einstellungen an Stereo-Decodern;* Funk-Technik, Vol. **19** (1964), No. 1, p. 23-24
[52] N. N., *Gesamtkatalog industrie elektronik* '66; Philips Industrie Elektronik GmbH, Hamburg, 1965
[53] G. W. Schanz, *Ein denkendes Röhrenvoltmeter;* Deutsches Elektrohandwerk, Vol. **40** (1965), No. 5, p. 147-148
[54] J. Czech, *Oscilloscope measuring technique*, Philips Technical Library, Eindhoven 1965
[55] J. Czech, *Fortschritte auf dem Gebiet der Elektronenstrahl-Oszillografen;* in: Handbuch für Hochfrequenz- und Elektro-Techniker, Vol. VII; Verlag für Radio-Foto-Kinotechnik GmbH, Berlin, 1964
[56] H. J. Burema and J. poole, *Largely transistorized* PM 3230 *double-beam oscilloscope;* electronic measuring and microwave notes, No. 1/1964, p. 1-2; N.V. Philips' Gloeilampenfabrieken, Eindhoven

[57] A. Bouwens, *A generator for the FM stereo system;* electronic measuring and microwave notes, No. 1/1964, p. 8; N.V. Philips 'Gloeilampenfabrieken, Eindhoven

INDEX

PHILIPS PAPERBACKS

- This is a series covering subjects in all branches of radio and electronics.
- Typical subjects covered are radio technology, audio fidelity, radio and television transmitting and receiving problems, tape recorders, DC relays, aerials, short wave reception, transistors in logical circuits, and electronic measuring devices.
- Written for both the technician and the student.
- Many titles to suit the keen amateur and the interested layman.
- Lavishly illustrated.

Already published in this series:

P 1 G. SLOT: **AUDIO QUALITY**

Requirements for high quality audio equipment.

VIII + 156 pages, 61 line drawings and 26 tables. 13s.6d. net.

This book deals with the problem of obtaining the quality of sound reproduction that will give the maximum satisfaction to those listening to it. The author considers the whole problem objectively. A chapter spent on discussing the "problem" is followed by one on the technical specifications. This leads on to one on loudness level and power requirements. Then follow successively chapters on non-linear distortion, frequency response, pitch deviation, and background noises. Two chapters are then devoted respectively to stereophony and ambiophony, and finally the author deals with the classification of systems and the use of equipment.

P 2 C. G. NIJSEN: **THE TAPE RECORDER**

A complete handbook on magnetic recording.

X + 142 pages, 57 line drawings and 30 pages of plates, one a fold-out, on art paper. 13s.6d. net.

With this book, the reader wishing to make his own recordings can familiarise himself in a systematic way with both the theoretical and practical sides of this intriguing subject. At his disposal are the author's experience and extensive knowledge of the applications of the tape recorder, gained in professional sound studios and as an adjudicator at sound contests. Above all, this is a practical book on an aspect of electronics now in the forefront of public interest.

Contents include:

What is sound? - sound recording and reproduction - the tape recorder - acoustics - stereophony - choosing a recorder - advice on making recordings - applications of the tape recorder from A to Z - the recorder in general education and the study of music-tape clubs and sound recording as a hobby - dictation machines - magnetic recording conquers the world.

P 3 D. J. W. SJOBBEMA: **AERIALS**

TV and FM receiving aerials.

VIII + 110 pages, 98 line drawings. 10s.6d. net.

Such things as high sensitivity and good-quality reproduction from a receiver deserve an aerial both correctly designed and erected. In addition to discussing the principles of aerial technology, the book deals fully with the many practical aspects of aerial arrays. The reader will find here not only many designs, but also solutions to those problems confronting every aerial erector.

Contents include:

The energy transfer from emitter to receiver - the receiving aerial - the choice and installation of the aerial - connecting the aerial to the receiver - attenuators - several receivers connected to the same aerial.

RADIO SERVICING

Radio Servicing comprises a total of six books which together form a manual on the repair of radio receivers. All are written in simple language.

Each books deals with a specific subject and each chapter is followed by a short summary, together with a number of questions designed to test the reader's grasp of what he has read.
Theoretical principles are treated only where absolutely necessary. Clear insight is given into the functioning of a radio receiver, interpretation of technical diagrams, the use of measuring apparatus, tracing and repairing the most common faults, etc.

P 4 EDGAR J. BLACK: **DIRECT CURRENT AND MAGNETISM**

VIII + 119 pages, 92 line drawings. 10s.6d. net.

P 5 EDGAR J. BLACK: **ALTERNATING CURRENT AND ACOUSTICS**

VIII + 116 pages, 86 line drawings. 10s.6d. net.

P 6 EGDAR J. BLACK: **RADIO VALVES**

VIII + 126 pages, 90 line drawings. 10s.6d. net.

P 7 EDGAR J. BLACK: **A. F. AMPLIFICATION**

VIII + 109 pages, 82 line drawings. 10s.6d. net.

Other titles in Radio Servicing in preparation:

P 8 MEASURING INSTRUMENTS

P 9 FAULT-FINDING IN RADIO RECEIVERS

P 10 A. H. RUINSMA: **CIRCUITS USING DIRECT CURRENT RELAYS**

IX + 86 pages, 66 line drawings. 13s.6d. net.

This book gives an insight into a number of uncommon circuits which have already proved themselves in practice and the possibility of applying direct current relays in commanded or programmed sequency circuits is fully explained.

Contents include:

General data of relays for direct current supply - operation of a relay - retarding a relay - short-term relay operation - operating a relay by means of physical phenomena - commanded sequence circuits - automatic sequence circuits with commanded start - oscillating circuits - some special circuits.

P 11 J. Ph. KORTHALS ALTES: **TRANSISTORS IN LOGICAL CIRCUITS**

VIII + 117 pages, 125 line drawings and 2 plates. 16s. net.

Starting from already known analogue relay circuits, this book describes in a special way the logical electronic circuits using semiconductors.

Contents include:

Some concepts of switch algebra - the twofold or binary system - the transistor as a switch - diodes - AND-, OR and NOT operation with semiconductors - signal amplification - bistable stages - multivibrators - counting switching circuits - arithmetical operations - observations - examples of applications - practical hints.

P 12 P. W. van der WAL: **LOUDSPEAKERS AND LOUDSPEAKER CABINETS**

VIII + 110 pages, 156 line drawings and 3 plates. 15s. net.

Besides providing particulars of numerous different speaker boxes, this book is a source of information on various matters, which although apparently incidental, must nevertheless be given due consideration if the best results are to be obtained. To enable the "do-it-yourself" enthusiast to deal with certain problems which may arise during the construction of the boxes, a chapter of practical hints is also included.

P 13 J. VASTENHOUD: **SHORT WAVE LISTENING**

VII + 120 pages, 33 line drawings and 4 plates. 12s.6d. net.

The book, which deals with the possibilities and problems of short-wave reception on the level of popular science will enable the reader to discover a whole new world of his own.

Contents include:

Short waves - the principles of short wave transmission - practical short wave transmitting - short wave prediction - sources of interference - the aerial - the correct choice of receiver - communications receivers - do any regulations exist governing the use of frequencies in the short wave band - DX-ing in practice. - DX-ing with a tape recorder - DX-ing using a frequency meter.

P 14 T. POTMA: **STRAIN GAUGES**

Theory and application

VIII + 139 pages, 135 line drawings and 30 photographs. 21s. net.

The book is primarily intended to assist those who have to deal with stress and strain measurements although they themselves are not very familiar with this field. It fills a gap which exist between the often highly specialised technical literature in existence and the brochures circulated by the manufacturers of strain gauges.

Contents include:

Types, design and manufacturing methods - characteristic quantities - measuring methods and equipment - compensation methods - basic strain-gauge techniques - applications of strain gauges - data